Direct Hits Toughest Vocabulary of the SAT: Volume 2

By Larry Krieger

Edited by Ted Griffith

This copy belongs to:

_____

For more information, contact us at:

Direct Hits Publishing
2639 Arden Rd., Atlanta GA 30327
Info@DirectHitsEducation.com

Visit our website at:
www.DirectHitsEducation.com

First Edition: August 2008

ISBN 10:   0-981-81841-2

ISBN 13:   978-0-9818184-1-2

Library of Congress Control Number: 2008906526

Edited by Ted Griffith

Cover Design by Carlo da Silva

Interior Design by Katherine Goodman

Acknowledgements

This book would not have been possible without the help of great students, dedicated friends and a tireless Product Manager. I would like to thank the following students for their valuable suggestions: Jacob Byrne, Jill Reid, Lindsey Brenner, Misha Milijanic, and Britney Frankel. Special thanks to Lauren Treene, Evan Hewel, Holland McTyeire and Alex Washington for their ability to help me connect vivid movie scenes with difficult SAT words.

I would also like to thank Jane Armstrong for her unfailing enthusiasm and Jan Altman for her original research. Extra special thanks to Claire Griffith for her encouragement and creative ideas and to Luther Griffith for his keen insights and impeccable judgment.

This book would not have been possible without a dedicated Product Manager. Ted Griffith has been everything an author could ask for - resourceful, innovative and meticulous.

And finally, I am deeply grateful for the "close reads," patience and love of my wife, Susan.

Table of Contents

Page

Introduction...i

About Larry Krieger.................................... iii

Chapter 6
Key Literary Terms:
191–205..1-10
Testing Your Vocabulary 11-17

Chapter 7
Key Words from Science and The Social Sciences:
206–250...19-45
Testing Your Vocabulary 46-51

Chapter 8
Words With Multiple Meanings:
251–265...53-61
Testing Your Vocabulary 62-68

Chapter 9
The Toughest Words I:
266–315.. 69-91
Testing Your Vocabulary 92-96

Chapter 10:
The Toughest Words II:
316–365.. 97-120
Testing Your Vocabulary 121-126

Final Review.. 127-137

Fast Review 139-150

Index 151-159

Introduction

Most students believe that learning new words is a tedious chore that involves memorizing long lists of "big" but useless vocabulary words. Like Volume 1, this book is designed to provide you with a new and different approach to learning challenging vocabulary.

Volume 2 features 175 words that have all appeared on recent SATs. Each of these words is illustrated with an ECLECTIC (varied) mix of examples taken from pop culture, historic events and contemporary issues. For example, you'll discover that the French king Louis XIV and the American rapper 50 Cent share a PENCHANT (liking) for ORNATE (lavish) decorations while Queen Elizabeth I and Rick "The Big Boss" Ross share a passion for OSTENTATIOUS (showy) jewelry. You'll also learn about a PRISTINE (pure, untouched) rain forest, a PROLIFIC (very productive) NFL scorer and a PROVISIONAL (temporary) planet that was "plutoed!"

Volume 2 is designed to tackle challenging words that often appear in Level 4 and Level 5 questions. We begin with 15 literary terms and 45 words taken from the sciences and social sciences. These 60 academic words all appear in your textbooks and on the SAT.

Our next chapter defines and illustrates 15 words that look familiar but have multiple meanings. These everyday words such as FLAG, CHECK and COIN have surprising secondary meanings that can trick unsuspecting students.

Introduction

The final two chapters focus upon the 100 toughest words on the SAT. Each of these words has appeared as an answer or answer choice to a Level 5 question. Learning these words is guaranteed to raise your Critical Reading score.

I hope you enjoy learning the vocabulary words in Volume 2. I also want you to test your ability to use these words. Each SAT includes 48 critical reading questions and 19 sentence completion questions. Chapter 6 concludes with a set of 5 critical reading questions. You'll find a set of 10 sentence completion questions at the end of Chapters 7 - 10. In addition, Volume 2 concludes with a Final Review that contains 10 more sentence completion questions and 5 more critical reading questions. Taken together, the 60 questions in this volume will give you an opportunity to test your vocabulary on SAT questions.

So what are you waiting for? Louis XIV, 50 Cent, Queen Elizabeth I, Rick Ross and a host of superheroes, celebrities and historic figures are all waiting and eager to help you augment your vocabulary and raise your Critical Reading score!

About Larry Krieger

Larry Krieger is one of the foremost SAT experts in the country. His renowned teaching methods and SAT prep courses are praised for both their inventive, engaging approaches and their results. Students under Krieger's guidance improve their SAT scores by an average of 200 points.

Formerly a social studies supervisor and AP Art History teacher at New Jersey's SAT powerhouse Montgomery Township High School near Princeton, Krieger led the school to a Number 1 ranking in the state and nation for a comprehensive public high school. In 2004, Montgomery students achieved a record national average score of 629 on the Critical Reading section of the SAT.

Beginning in 2005, the College Board recognized Krieger's AP Art History course as the "strongest in the world" for three straight years. With an open enrollment, 60% of the senior class took the course and 100% made grades of 3 or higher, including some special education students.

Krieger is the co-author of several US History, World History and AP Art History texts used throughout the country. He earned a BA in History and an MAT from University of North Carolina at Chapel Hill, and has an MA in Sociology from Wake Forest.

Though Krieger admits to being completely unprepared for his first SAT in high school, he regularly takes the SAT to keep up with changes on the new test.

Chapter 6

KEY LITERARY TERMS: 191–205

Many students believe that literary terms such as SYNOPSIS, ANECDOTE, and ALLUSION are limited to language arts classes and tests. Nothing could be further from the truth. We often tell our friends summaries of favorite television shows, describe humorous incidents and make brief references to people and events. Literary terms are part of our everyday life. SAT test writers are also aware of the importance of literary terms. As a result, most exams include questions designed to determine if you can recognize IRONY, METAPHORICAL language and literary CARICATURES. This chapter defines and illustrates 15 frequently tested literary terms. As you study each term in this chapter try to think of additional examples from your reading and daily life.

191. SYNOPSIS:

A brief summary of the major points of a thesis, theory, story or literary work; an abstract; a PRÉCIS

Has anyone ever asked you to summarize a movie, television show, or a You Tube clip? If you did, you provided them with a SYNOPSIS or brief summary. Here is a SYNOPSIS of the movie "The Bourne Ultimatum": Jason Bourne dodges police, escapes Interpol and evades assassins as he searches for answers to his true identity.

192. SIMILE:

A figure of speech, often introduced by 'like' or 'as', which compares two unlike things

Here are some examples of SIMILES:

- I can hear sweat trickling down your cheek
  Your heartbeat sounds like Sasquatch feet
  Thundering, shaking the concrete.
  ~ Notorious B.I.G.

- Death lies on her, like an untimely frost.
  ~ William Shakespeare

- The apple-green car with the white vinyl roof and Florida plates turned into the street like a greased cobra.
  ~ Gloria Naylor

- You know the type, loud as a motor bike
  But wouldn't bust a grape in a fruit fight.
  ~ Jay-Z

193. METAPHOR:
A figure of speech in which a comparison is made between two unrelated objects

Metaphors have been used in written language since the dawn of recorded history. Here is an example from the "Epic of Gilgamesh":

My friend, the swift mule, fleet wild ass of the mountain, panther of the wilderness, after we joined together and went up into the mountain, fought the Bull of Heaven and killed it, and overwhelmed Humbaba, who lived in the Cedar Forest, now what is this sleep that has seized you?

In this passage, the friend is compared to a mule, a wild ass, and a panther to indicate that the speaker sees traits from these animals in his friend.

The use of METAPHORS did not stop with the ancient Sumerians. In "High School Musical 2," Taylor warns Gabriella to watch out for the ever-devious Sharpay by saying, "that girl's got more moves than an octopus in a wrestling match."

194. IRONY:
A form of speech in which what we say or write conveys the opposite of its literal meaning

IRONY involves the perception that things are not what they are said to be or what they seem.

Here are some examples of IRONY:

- In "Star Wars," Han Solo tells Jabba the Hutt, "Jabba, you're a wonderful human being." Jabba is, in fact, neither wonderful nor a human being!

- In Shakespeare's *Julius Caesar*, Marc Antony gives a famous IRONIC speech in which he repeats "And Brutus is an honorable man," when Brutus has just killed Julius Caesar and is not honorable at all!

- In Sophocles' *Oedipus Rex* it is IRONIC that Oedipus thinks he is the detective in finding out who killed his predecessor, when he is actually, IRONICALLY, the murderer.

195. SATIRE:
   A work that ridicules human vices and follies; comic criticism

What do the television program "The Office" and the movie "WALL-E" have in common? Both make extensive use of SATIRE to ridicule human follies. "The Office" provides razor-sharp SATIRE of unmotivated cubicle workers and clueless bosses such as Michael Scott. In one episode, Scott orders his employees to paste ethnic labels on their foreheads and then try to guess their identities.

The movie "WALL-E" SATIRIZES human folly by showing how out-of-control human consumption left Earth covered with enormous piles of trash. Meanwhile, humans live on a gigantic spaceship where they spend endless days sipping meals out of a cup as they recline on floating easy chairs. The humans depicted in "WALL-E" are CORPULENT (overweight) and have REGRESSED (moved backwards) to a baby-like appearance with chubby extremities and little bone density.

196. HYPERBOLE:

A figure of speech in which exaggeration is used for emphasis or effect; extreme exaggeration

Have you ever exaggerated something to make a point? Everyone does. In show business these exaggerations are called hype. In literature and daily life they are called HYPERBOLES.

Here is a list of some commonly used HYPERBOLES:

- "I'm so tired that I could sleep for a year."
- "I'm so hungry that I could eat a horse."
- "This book weighs a ton."

197. CARICATURE:

A representation in which the subject's distinctive features or peculiarities are deliberately exaggerated to produce a comic effect.

Do you look at the editorial cartoons in your local newspaper? Editorial cartoonists often incorporate CARICATURES of political figures into their cartoons. For example, Thomas Nast's CARICATURES of Boss Tweed helped to focus public attention on the Tweed Ring's corrupt practices. Modern cartoonists often CARICATURE Jay Leno, the host of *The Tonight Show*, by exaggerating his already prominent chin.

198. EPIC:

A long narrative poem written in a grand style to celebrate the feats of a legendary hero

SAGA:

A long narrative story; a heroic tale

Both EPICS and SAGAS are long and both feature the feats of heroes. The two literary forms differ in that an EPIC is a narrative poem and a SAGA is a narrative story written in prose.

The *Iliad* is the first and greatest EPIC in Western literature. Other famous EPICS include Virgil's *Aeneid*, Homer's *The Odyssey* and Milton's *Paradise Lost*. J.K. Rowling's series of seven Harry Potter novels provide a contemporary example of a literary SAGA while George Lucas' six Star Wars films provide a contemporary example of a cinematic SAGA.

199. EUPHONY:

Soothing or pleasant sounds; harmonious

CACOPHONY:

Harsh clashing sounds; jarring; grating

In their classic Motown song, "My Girl," The Temptations tell everyone who will listen that "I've got a sweeter song than the birds in the trees. Well I guess you'd say what can make me feel this way? My girl, talkin' 'bout my girl." The Temptations' soothing words and harmonious melody create a EUPH-ONIOUS sound. In contrast, Eminem describes his apprehension and fear before a make or break performance: "His palms are sweaty, knees weak, arms heavy. There's vomit on his sweater already, mom's spaghetti." Eminem's harsh grating words and rapid-fire rhythm create a CACOPHONOUS sound.

EUPHONY and CACOPHONY are easy words to learn. Both include the Greek root *phone* meaning sound (like a cell phone). Since the prefix *eu* means "good," EUPHONY literally means "good sound." Since the prefix *kakos* means "bad," CACOPHONY means "bad sound."

200. FORESHADOW:
To suggest or indicate that something will happen in a story; PRESAGE (Word 286)

The conclusion of "Batman Begins" FORESHADOWS the Caped Crusader's coming battle with the Joker. As the film ends, Lieutenant Gordon unveils a Bat-Signal for Batman. He then mentions a criminal who, like Batman, has "a taste for the theatrical," leaving a Joker playing card at his crime scenes. Batman promises to investigate it, thus PRESAGING his coming confrontation with the Joker in "The Dark Knight."

201. SUBPLOT:
A secondary plot in fiction or drama

Subplots are a common feature in novels and movies. For example, *The Great Gatsby* includes a SUBPLOT based upon the relationship between the narrator Nick Carraway and Jordan Baker, an attractive but CAPRICIOUS (Word 63) professional golfer. Similarly, the movie "Iron-Man" includes a SUBPLOT hinting at a possible future romance between Tony Stark and his loyal assistant "Pepper" Potts.

202. MEMOIR:
An autobiography; personal journal

What do President Ulysses S. Grant, rapper 50 Cent and rocker Anthony Kiedis have in common? All three wrote CANDID (open, honest) MEMOIRS describing their lives and careers. Written to pay off debts and provide for his family, the *Personal Memoirs of Ulysses S. Grant* is now considered the first and best presidential memoir. *From Pieces to Weight* is 50 Cent's unflinching MEMOIR chronicling his rise from Jamaica, Queens to the top of the Billboard charts. *Scar Tissue* is Anthony Kiedis' account of his career as the lead singer of the Red Hot Chili Peppers.

203. ANECDOTE
A short account of an interesting or humorous incident

What do the world-renowned physicist Albert Einstein and the lead singer of the Red Hot Chili Peppers Anthony Kiedis have in common? Both are very good at telling interesting ANECDOTES. In the following ANECDOTES Einstein provides a humorous explanation of relatively, and Kiedis provides a revealing ANECDOTE of what it is like to be the opening act for the Rolling Stones:

> Albert Einstein was often asked to explain the general theory of relativity. "Put your hand on a hot stove for a minute, and it seems like an hour," he once declared. "Sit with a pretty girl for an hour, and it seems like a minute. That's relativity."

"Opening for the Stones is a crummy job...First you get there and they won't let you do a sound check. Then they give you an eightieth of the stage. They set aside this tiny area and say, 'This is for you. You don't get the lights, and you're not allowed to use our sound system. And oh, by the way, you see that wooden floor? That's Mick's imported antique wood flooring from the Brazilian jungle, and that's what he dances on. If you so much as look at it, you won't get paid.'"

204. EULOGY:

A laudatory speech or written tribute, especially one praising someone who has died

Here are three noteworthy EULOGIES:

- Mark Antony's fictional EULOGY for Julius Caesar in Shakespeare's play *Julius Caesar*

- Ossie Davis's EULOGY for Malcolm X

- Earl Spencer's eulogy for Diana, Princess of Wales

On the lighter side, in the movie "Zoolander," Derek Zoolander delivered a EULOGY for his friends who died in the "Orange Mocha Frappuccino" gas fight.

205. ALLUSION:

An indirect or brief reference to a person, event, place, phrase, piece of art, or literary work that assumes a common knowledge with the reader or listener

Everyone uses ALLUSIONS. They form a shorthand for describing people, places, and events, and are drawn from a variety of sources. For example, the two numbers 9/11 are an ALLUSION to the terrorist attacks that occurred on September 11, 2001. A "Mona Lisa" smile is an ALLUSION to Leonardo da Vinci's famous, ENIGMATIC (Word 42) portrait. A "Catch 22" situation refers to the type of problem in Joseph Heller's novel *Catch 22* in which there is no right answer. The poems in your literature classes also contain ALLUSIONS. For example, Robert Frost's famous poem "The Road Not Taken" uses a traveler's choice of which trail to follow as an ALLUSION to the inevitable decisions we have to make in life.

Testing Your Vocabulary

Each SAT contains 19 sentence completion questions and 48 critical reading questions. While the words in this chapter are used infrequently in sentence completions, they often appear in critical reading questions. Always remember that each passage will contain key words and phrases that will lead you to the correct answer. Use the vocabulary from Chapter 6 to answer the following 5 critical reading questions and make sure to circle your answers. You'll find answers and explanations on pages 16-17.

While critics panned Laurie's essays as too arcane for the average reader, they rushed to praise Madison's new novel. According to her legion of adoring fans, Madison writes in a hip, contemporary style, full of topical pop culture references. Thus, she writes knowingly about Miley Cyrus' latest song, Patrick Dempsey's latest movie and Rick Ross' latest chain and piece. As a result, Madison is being universally praised as a promising new talent.

1. Lines 5 – 8 ("Thus, she ... piece") serve to provide examples of

 (A) particular references that critics found too esoteric
 (B) diverse subjects about which Madison has only superficial knowledge
 (C) comic subplots that enhance the novel's core theme
 (D) anecdotes that illustrate key ideas
 (E) specific allusions in Madison's novel

In the movie, "300," director Zach Snyder compares Sparta to a lonely citadel of freedom valiantly holding out against the tyrant Xerxes and his vast horde of Persian soldiers. This heroic image of indomitable Spartans determined to fight to the death remains dominant in popular culture. Without slighting Sparta's contribution to the defense of ancient Greece, it is important to remember that it was the Athenians who sacrificed their city and then defeated the Persian fleet at the watershed battle of Platea.

2. The author suggests that the "lonely citadel of freedom" (line 2) is best understood as

   (A) an anecdote relaying an important message
   (B) an unflattering flashback
   (C) a vivid metaphor for heroic resistance
   (D) a satirical commentary on Spartan bravery
   (E) an uninspired simile

In her novel, *The Women of Brewster Place*, Gloria Naylor describes Etta Johnson's deliberately conspicuous arrival at Brewster Place: "The apple-green car with the white vinyl roof and Florida plates turned into the street like a greased cobra. Since Etta had stopped at a Mobil station three blocks away to work off the evidence of a hot, dusty 1,200-mile odyssey home, the chrome caught the rays of the afternoon sun and shone brightly like a gaudy neon sign."

3. Lines 3 – 8 ("The apple-green...sign")are notable for their use of

    (A)   wry wit
    (B)   vivid similes
    (C)   biting satire
    (D)   obscure allusions
    (E)   illuminating anecdotes

As a young boy, I beamed with pride as college students described my father's economics lectures. Everyone praised his vivid anecdotes, amusing stories and vast storehouse of economic data that he could marshal at a moment's notice. The "Professor," as everyone called him, even appeared as a guest pundit on a local television program. The first time I saw dad I was shocked and embarrassed. The bright lights and heavy makeup exaggerated his bushy eyebrows and lit up his bald head. The same darting eyes that mesmerized his students gave him the appearance of one of the villains I watched on the Sunday morning cartoon shows.

4. In lines 6 – 12 ("The first time ... shows"), the narrator suggests that, on television his father came across as a

    (A) caricature
    (B) knowledgeable commentator
    (C) self-deprecating authority
    (D) ironic and tragic figure
    (E) raconteur

Mr. Williams praised Alex's short story for its descriptive vocabulary and impressive use of metaphorical language. However, as an honest and incisive critic, Mr. Williams admonished Alex for failing to explore the relationship between the literal meaning of what his protagonist said and what he really implied.

5.   Mr. Williams criticized Alex's short story for its

   (A)   outstanding use of metaphors and similes
   (B)   magisterial tone
   (C)   incoherent structure
   (D)   lack of dramatic irony
   (E)   unrealistic hyperboles

Answers and Explanations

1. **E**

   An ALLUSION (Word 205) is an indirect or brief reference to a person, place or event. The passage notes that Madison's writing is filled with examples of "topical pop culture references." Since these references are specific allusions, the correct answer is E, "specific allusions in Madison's novel."

2. **C**

   A METAPHOR (Word 193) is a figure of speech comparing two unlike things. Director Zack Snyder compares Sparta to a "lonely citadel of freedom valiantly holding out against the tyrant Xerxes..." The correct answer is therefore C, "a vivid metaphor for heroic resistance."

3. **B**

   A SIMILE (Word 192) is a figure of speech using like or as to compare two unlike things. Gloria Naylor uses similes when she writes that the Etta's car was "like a greased cobra" and that the car's chrome "shone brightly like a gaudy neon sign." The correct answer is therefore B, "vivid similes."

4. **A**

   A CARICATURE (Word 197) is a deliberately exaggerated portrait. The key word "exaggerates" signals that the description of the narrator's father is in fact a caricature. The correct answer is therefore A, "caricature."

5.   **D**

IRONY (Word 194) is used to describe a situation in which things are not what they are said to be or what they seem. Mr. Williams criticized Alex for not fully exploring "the discrepancy between the literal meaning of what his protagonists said and what he really implied." Mr. Williams thus underscored Alex's failure to use dramatic irony. The correct answer is therefore D, "lack of dramatic irony."

Chapter 7

KEY WORDS FROM SCIENCE AND THE SOCIAL SCIENCES: 206–250

Many students believe that SAT words are obscure and rarely used by anyone except test writers at the Educational Testing Service. Nothing could be further from the truth. Newspapers, magazines, and Internet blogs frequently use SAT vocabulary words. Front page headlines describe "watershed events," financial articles discuss "lucrative deals," and editorials urge politicians to "reach a consensus" on important issues.

This chapter highlights 45 key words taken from science and the social sciences. While all appear on the SAT, they are also all everyday words that you encounter in school and on the internet. Since memorizing lists is inefficient and ineffective, we have provided vivid examples designed to help you make a permanent connection with each word.

A. SCIENCE: THESE WORDS WILL HELP YOU DESCRIBE WHAT IS HAPPENING IN THE SCIENCE LAB

206. CATALYST:

In chemistry, a CATALYST is a substance (such as an enzyme) that accelerates the rate of a chemical reaction at some temperature, but without itself being transformed or consumed by the reaction. In everyday usage a CATALYST is any agent that provokes or triggers change.

Both Rosa Parks and Rachel Carson were CATALYSTS whose actions helped provoke historic changes. Rosa Parks' refusal to give up her bus seat acted as a CATALYST that helped spark the Montgomery Bus Boycott. Today, Rosa Parks is hailed as one of the pioneers of the modern civil rights movement. Rachel Carson's book *Silent Spring* was a CATALYST that triggered a national campaign to limit the indiscriminate use of DDT and other harmful pesticides. Today, Rachel Carson is hailed as one of the pioneers of the modern environmental movement.

207. CAUSTIC:

In chemistry, a CAUSTIC substance is one that burns or destroys organic tissue by chemical action. Hydro fluoric acid and silver nitrate are examples of CAUSTIC substances. In everyday usage, a CAUSTIC comment is one that hurts or burns.

In the movie "Ever After," Danielle asked her wicked step-mother, "Was there ever a time, even in its smallest measure, when you loved me?" The insensitive step-mother replied, "How can anyone love a pebble in their shoe?" Ouch! Now that was a CAUSTIC remark!

Simon Cowell is a judge on "American Idol" who is famous for the CAUSTIC criticisms he directs at INEPT (unskilled) contestants. For example, he told one would-be singer, "If your life guard duties were as good as your singing, a lot of people would be drowning." Ouch! Now that was a CAUSTIC remark!

208. SYNTHETIC:
Produced artificially, especially in a laboratory or other man-made environment

SYNTHETIC fibers such as nylon and polyester are a familiar part of our everyday lives. Nylon fibers are used to make everything from bridal veils to carpets. Reebok, Nike and UnderArmour all use polyester to make form-fitting, moisture-wicking compression shorts and sweat pants.

While we take all these products for granted, a new SYNTHETIC swimsuit has raised a number of controversial issues. In February 2008, Speedo unveiled its new LZR Racer full-body swimsuit. The Racer is made out of a microfiber woven from chlorine resistant elastics and ultra fine nylon thread. The SYNTHETIC suit is ultra light, water repellent and extremely fast. Since its introduction scores of world records have been broken by swimmers using the suit. But critics equate the suit with taking performance enhancing steroids. They charge that it should be banned because it gives some swimmers an unfair competitive advantage.

209. OSMOSIS:

In chemistry, OSMOSIS refers to the diffusion of a fluid through a semi-permeable membrane until there is an equal concentration of fluid on both sides of the membrane. In everyday usage, OSMOSIS refers to a gradual, often unconscious process of assimilation.

What do students studying for the SAT and the Holy Roman Emperor Charlemagne have in common? Charlemagne valued education and tried so hard to study Latin that he had tablets with vocabulary words placed under his pillow. Charlemagne apparently hoped he could learn difficult words by OSMOSIS. Like Charlemagne, modern SAT students have to learn difficult new words. But, don't put this book under your pillow. OSMOSIS didn't work for Charlemagne and it won't work for you! The words in this book can only be learned by studying and using them.

210. SEDENTARY:

In ecology, animals that are SEDENTARY remain or live in one area. In everyday usage, SEDENTARY means settled and therefore accustomed to sitting or doing little exercise

What do fungus beetles and the humans in the movie "WALL-E" have in common? Both live SEDENTARY lives. Fungus beetles are SEDENTARY creatures that seldom move more than a few yards between fungi, their primary food. The humans in "WALL-E" are twenty-eighth century couch potatoes who spend most of their time reclining in chairs while staring at computer screens. As a result of this SEDENTARY life style, the humans are obese and have almost lost the ability to walk.

211. VIRULENT:

In medical science, VIRULENT refers to a disease or toxin that is extremely infectious, malignant or poisonous. In everyday usage, VIRULENT refers to language that is bitterly hostile, hateful, and antagonistic

What do the blue-ringed octopus and the hook-nosed sea snake have in common? Both are DIMINUTIVE (Word 51) animals whose venom is extremely VIRULENT. Although only the size of a golf ball, the blue-ringed octopus can kill an adult human in minutes with its VIRULENT venom. Armed with venom four to eight times more VIRULENT than that of a cobra, the hook-nosed sea snake can easily kill almost any animal that encroaches on its territory.

The blue-ringed octopus and the hook-nosed sea snake use their VIRULENT venom to protect themselves from predators. In contrast, Al Qaeda terrorists regularly broadcast VIRULENT speeches directed at the innocent citizens of democratic nations.

212. EMPIRICAL:

In science, EMPIRICAL means originating in or based on direct observation and experience. EMPIRICAL data can then be used to support or reject a hypothesis. In everyday language, EMPIRICAL means to be guided by practical experience, not theory.

The process of applying to colleges can be a DAUNTING (intimidating) challenge. You should begin your search with a series of questions: Would you prefer to go to an urban college or one in a more BUCOLIC (Word 79) setting? Would you be more comfortable in a large state university or a small private college? These questions are only a first step. It is very important to be EMPIRICAL, to gather facts. Don't speculate about what a college is like or what test scores you will need. Be an EMPIRICIST and visit a number of colleges. On your visit gather EMPIRICAL information by visiting dorms, observing classes, talking with students and, above all, asking questions.

213. ENTOMOLOGY:

The scientific study of insects

How are honeybees, strawberry ice cream, ENTOMOLOGISTS and the SAT connected? Honeybees are responsible for pollinating one-third of all the foods we eat including strawberries, blueberries, apples, almonds, and melons. Without honeybees, all-natural strawberry ice cream would be impossible to make. The last several winters have witnessed the sudden disappearance of more than 25 percent of the Western honeybee population.

ENTOMOLOGISTS are MYSTIFIED (baffled) by what is officially called colony collapse disorder. While SAT test writers may or may not be aware of the problem facing honeybees, they are aware that many students confuse ENTOMOLOGY with ETYMOLOGY. ENTOMOLOGY is the study of insects while ETYMOLOGY is a branch of linguistics concerned with the history of words.

214. GESTATE:

In science, GESTATE means to carry within the uterus from conception to delivery. In everyday language, GESTATE means to conceive and develop in the mind

Periods of GESTATION vary from animal to animal. For example, the period of GESTATION for domestic-ated cats and dogs is 2 months. In contrast, the period of GESTATION for elephants is almost 22 months!

Ideas, like a fetus, often require time to GESTATE. For example, the ideas contained in the Declaration of Independence did not suddenly spring from Jefferson's mind onto a piece of parchment. He later acknow-ledged that his eloquent statements about natural rights were derived from the English philosopher John Locke and had been GESTATING in his mind for some time.

215. PARADIGM:

In science, a PARADIGM is a framework or model of thought

Have you ever stood still and looked at the sky? Doesn't it seem obvious that the Earth stays in one place while everything in the sky rises, sets or goes around it? These seemingly obvious observations led Ptolemy, a second century astronomer, to formulate the geocentric PARADIGM that the earth is the center of the solar system. However, "obvious" observations are not always true. In 1543, Copernicus formulated a new heliocentric PARADIGM that correctly placed the sun at the center of the solar system.

Ptolemy's ERRONEOUS (inaccurate) PARADIGM illustrates the point that obvious observations do not always lead to the best framework of thought. For example, many students use an ineffective SAT guessing PARADIGM based upon the belief that it is best to guess on any question they don't know. This PARADIGM fails to account for ALLURING (enticing) wrong answers and a "guessing penalty" that results in the loss of .25 points for every wrong answer. A more effective test-taking PARADIGM begins with these three PRAGMATIC (Word 12) questions: First, which college do you want to go to? Second, what SAT scores do you need to be accepted into these colleges? And third, how many questions do you need to correctly answer to achieve this score? For example, a student striving for a Critical Reading score of 650 must correctly answer 53 or 54 of the 67 questions. This PRAGMATIC PARADIGM gives you a framework for guessing by telling you how many questions you can skip and still achieve your goal score.

B.   ECONOMICS: THESE   WORDS   ARE ABOUT DOLLARS AND SENSE

216. ENTREPRENEUR
A person who organizes and manages a business or enterprise

What do Robert L. Johnson, Margaret Whitman and Richard Branson have in common? All three are successful ENTREPRENEURS who have become billionaires. Johnson displayed his ENTRE-PRENEURIAL talents by founding the Black Entertainment Television (BET) network and by becoming the first black majority owner of a major sports team, the NBA's Charlotte Bobcats. Whitman displayed her ENTREPRENEURIAL talents by transforming eBay from a small auction site with 30 employees and annual revenues of $4 million into an Internet titan with 15,000 employees and $8 billion in annual revenue. And Richard Branson displayed his ENTREPRENEURIAL talents by founding the Virgin Megastores and Virgin Atlantic Airways. Known for his PANACHE (Word 81) and enterprising spirit, Branson will soon unveil Virgin Galactic, a daring airline that will take INTREPID (Word 73) and AFFLUENT (Word 221) passengers into suborbital space with tickets priced at around $200,000.

217. LUCRATIVE
Very profitable

How are the drink Vitamin Water, the rapper 50 Cent and the SAT word LUCRATIVE connected? Vitamin Water is a popular drink owned by a company named Glacéau. 50 Cent invested in Glacéau in 2004 and owns 10 percent of the company. In July 2007, Coca Cola purchased Glacéau for $4.1 billion. As a result, 50 Cent earned over $400 million from the transaction! Now that was a LUCRATIVE investment!

218. EXTRAVAGANT:
Excessive and therefore lacking restraint.

What will 50 Cent do with the $400 million in profit he earned from his investment in Vitamin Water? Well, he can now purchase Three Ponds, one of the most expensive and EXTRAVAGANT homes in America. Located in Bridgehampton on Long Island, NY, Three Ponds is a 25,000 square-foot Italian villa that includes two three-car garages. Automated blinds, heated marble floors and a marble-surround spa tub make the master bedroom suite the perfect place to relax in luxury.

When he wants to enjoy nature, 50 Cent can stroll the 60 acre estate, play golf on its own 18 hole course and admire its 12 gardens and of course its beautiful three large ponds. What is the price for this EXTRAVAG-ANT home? A PRODIGIOUS (Word 20) $68 million!

219. AVARICE:
Excessive desire for material wealth; greedy; covetous

Philosophers and religious leaders have long con-demned AVARICE. The Greek philosopher Aristotle demonstrated his deep understanding of human nature when he wrote, "The AVARICE of mankind is insatiable." During the Middle Ages, Christian theologians identified AVARICE as one of the seven deadly sins. Sculptors often showed AVARICIOUS moneylenders being tortured by demons while clutching bags filled with coins.

While theologians have long denounced AVARICE, it does have defenders in the world of high finance. In the movie "Wall Street," Gordon Gekko was an AVARICIOUS corporate raider. He vigorously advocated AVARICE when he proclaimed, "greed is good. Greed works, greed is right ... Greed for life, money, love, knowledge, has marked the upward surge of mankind – and greed, mark my words, will save the malfunctioning corporation called the U.S.A."

220. GLUT, PLETHORA, SURFEIT:
A surplus

PAUCITY:
A shortage

Americans have traditionally purchased big cars, SUVs and pick-up trucks. However, as the price of gasoline began to soar, Americans turned to smaller, more fuel-efficient vehicles. Automakers were soon caught with a GLUT of SUVs and a PAUCITY of hybrids. As automobile manufacturers scrambled to produce more fuel-efficient models, used car lots had a SURFEIT of gas-guzzling vehicles and a DEARTH (Word 4) of buyers.

While our used car lots now have a GLUT of gas-guzzling vehicles, our landfills are filling up with a GLUT of old computers, printers, TVs and other unwanted consumer electronic goods. Americans are now throwing away 2 million tons of electronic trash, or e-waste, each year. While there is a SURFEIT of outdated e-waste, there is currently a PAUCITY of recycling options. The Environmental Protection Agency estimates that we only recycle 350,000 tons of e-waste each year.

221. DESTITUTE, IMPOVERISHED, INDIGENT:
Very poor

AFFLUENT and OPULENT:
Very wealthy

In the movie, "Trading Places," Eddie Murphy's character was originally DESTITUTE but became very AFFLUENT. In the movie, "Coming to America," Murphy played an African prince who pretended to be IMPOVERISHED but had in fact grown up in an OPULENT palace.

Eddie Murphy's characters were both fictional. In the movie "The Pursuit of Happyness," Will Smith portrayed the real life story of how Chris Gardner lost all of his family's savings by investing in a franchise selling bone density scanners. As a result, Chris became INDIGENT, forcing him and his young son to spend nights riding buses and sleeping in subway restrooms. Chris ultimately became AFFLUENT by learning how to become a successful stock broker.

222. MUNIFICENT:
Very generous

Americans responded to the Hurricane Katrina relief effort with an outpouring of generous contributions.

Led by MUNIFICENT contributions from Wal-Mart, Oprah Winfrey, Sean "Diddy" Combs, Celine Dion, Jay-Z, Hillary Duff, Morgan Freeman, Tim McGraw, NFL players and concerned citizens across America, billions of dollars were given to help revive New Orleans and the rest of the stricken Gulf Coast.

223. PARSIMONIOUS:
Excessively cheap with money; stingy

Which person would you want to be? A person who drives a luxury sports car, eats at expensive restaurants, owns all the latest electronic gadgets and lives paycheck-to-paycheck? Or a person who drives an older model car, reserves dining out for special occasions, doesn't bother with expensive electronic toys and has enough money saved in the bank and in investments to live for the rest of his or her life? The first person is self-INDULGENT (Word 57) while the second person is PARSIMONIOUS. Clearly both lifestyles have advantages and disadvantages. The self-INDULGENT lifestyle prizes HEDONISM (Word 104) but sacrifices security. The PARSIMONIOUS lifestyle prizes self-denial but sacrifices immediate gratification.

The most famous person renowned for his PARSIMONIOUS behavior is Ebenezer Scrooge, from Charles Dickens' *A Christmas Carol*. In fact, people who are PARSIMONIOUS are often called "Scrooges."

224. DEPRECIATION:
Any decrease or loss in value caused by age, wear, or market conditions

DEPRECIATION means that values are going down (remember that the prefix *de* means down). The stock market Crash of 1929 helped PRECIPITATE (Word 253) a severe DEPRECIATION in the value of stocks. By 1932, stocks listed on the New York Stock Exchange were worth just 11 percent of their pre-Crash value.

While the United States has not experienced an economic depression since the 1930s, DEPRECIATION can still be a serious economic problem. For example, beginning in 2007 there were too many homes for sale and not enough qualified buyers. As a result, home prices DEPRECIATED in value.

225. REMUNERATE:
To compensate; make payment for; to pay a person

REMUNERATION varies greatly from job to job. On July 24, 2008 the Federal minimum wage rose from $5.85 per hour to $6.55 per hour. The President of the United States earns $400,000 per year and the Vice-President earns $208,102. In contrast, NBA superstar LeBron James earns $30.8 million a year in salary and endorsements.

C. HISTORY AND GEOGRAPHY: THESE WORDS WILL HELP YOU UNDERSTAND PEOPLE, PLACES AND EVENTS

226. ACCORD:
A formal agreement

In "Pirates of the Caribbean: The Curse of the Black Pearl," Captain Jack Sparrow and Will reached an ACCORD. Will agreed to free Sparrow, and Sparrow agreed to help Will find Elizabeth. In world affairs, nations also reach ACCORDS. Signed on September 17, 1978, the Camp David ACCORDS provided a framework for establishing peaceful relations between Egypt and Israel.

227. ENLIGHTEN:
To inform, instruct, illuminate and thus remove darkness and ignorance

During the Enlightenment, writers such as Voltaire ENLIGHTENED European society by urging people to use science and reason instead of blindly following inherited prejudices. In cartoons and comics, why do you think a light-bulb appears over someone's head when the person suddenly understands something? Because they are ENLIGHTENED!

228. APPEASEMENT:
The policy of granting concessions to maintain peace

Would you APPEASE a crying child by giving him or her a piece of candy? Would you APPEASE a bully who threatened to beat you up? Are there times when APPEASEMENT is a wise policy? The British Prime Minister Neville Chamberlain thought so. At the Munich Conference in September 1938, Chamberlain APPEASED Hitler by agreeing to his demand to control the Sudetenland. When he returned to London, Chamberlain told cheering crowds, "I believe it is peace for our time." Chamberlain's prediction proved to be tragically wrong.

229. NULLIFY:
To make null; declare invalid

The tariffs of 1828 and 1832 infuriated John C. Calhoun of South Carolina. Led by Calhoun, South Carolina voted to NULLIFY or invalidate the tariffs. President Jackson rejected NULLIFICATION by saying it was treason and that those implementing it were traitors. The crisis was averted when Henry Clay devised a compromise in which the tariffs were gradually lowered.

230. TRIUMVIRATE:
A group or association of three leaders

John C. Calhoun, Henry Clay (See Word 229) and Daniel Webster were a group of three American statesmen known as "The Great Triumvirate," who dominated the U.S. Senate during the 1830s and 1840s. While the term TRIUMVIRATE usually refers to political leaders, it can be used to describe any group of three (remember, the prefix *tri* means three). For example, Michelangelo, Leonardo da Vinci and Raphael formed a TRIUMVIRATE of artists who dominated the High Renaissance. Today, the video game console market is dominated by the TRIUMVIRATE of Nintendo's Wii, Sony's PlayStation 3 and Microsoft's Xbox 360.

231. PRETEXT:
An excuse; an alleged cause

On August 2 and 4, 1964, two America destroyers patrolling international waters in the Gulf of Tonkin reported that they had been fired upon by North Vietnamese PT boats. While later investigations strongly suggested that the North Vietnamese fired in self-defense on August 2nd and that the "attack" of August 4th never happened, President Johnson used the alleged attacks as a PRETEXT to ask Congress for broader powers. The PRETEXT worked. Congress promptly passed the Tonkin Gulf Resolution giving Johnson a blank check to escalate the war in Southeast Asia.

The Vietnam War was not the only time that American presidents used a PRETEXT to justify military action. Although it is still unclear what caused the battleship *Maine* to explode, President McKinley used the incident as a PRETEXT to ask Congress for a declaration of war against Spain.

232. WATERSHED:
Critical point that marks a change of course; a turning point

Each generation of Americans has experienced a WATERSHED event that has riveted the entire nation and has marked a crucial historic turning point. Older

Americans, for example, can remember exactly where they were when they heard the tragic news that President Kennedy had been assassinated. Can you name a WATERSHED event that has taken place during your lifetime? Where were you, for example, when you heard about the 9/11 terrorist attacks?

233. CONSENSUS:
A general agreement

Do you think there is a need to develop and use more alternative energy sources? If you answer yes to this question you are part of a growing national CONSENSUS on this issue. Soaring gasoline prices have forced Americans to realize that we cannot indefinitely continue to import 70 percent of our oil at an annual cost of $700 billion. Note that a CONSENSUS does not mean that everyone must be in complete agreement with a policy or a decision. While there is a CONSENSUS that America must develop new sources of energy, there is not yet a CONSENSUS on which of the MYRIAD (Word 308) proposed alternative energy solutions should be utilized.

234. AUTOCRAT and DESPOT:
A ruler having unlimited power

In the movie "300," Xerxes is portrayed as an AUTOCRAT who is determined to conquer and enslave the freedom-loving Greeks. However, led by Sparta and Athens, the Greeks successfully defeat Xerxes thus defending democracy. Although democracy continues to make great strides, the modern world still has countries ruled by DESPOTS.

For example, Kim Jong Il wields absolute power over North Korea. Known to his people as "The Dear Leader," the AUTOCRATIC Kim brutally suppresses dissidents and maintains the world's 4th largest army. While his IMPOVERISHED (Word 221) people suffer from repeated famines, their DESPOTIC "Dear Leader" dines on steak and sips expensive imported wines.

235. MANIFESTO:

A public declaration of beliefs, policies or intentions

MANIFESTOS are not written by people who are self-satisfied and complacent. They are written by people who are INDIGNANT (Word 65) and who demand a change. For example, in 1848 a small but determined group of feminists held a Women's Rights Convention at Seneca Falls, New York. Led by the defiant Elizabeth Cady Stanton, they issued a MANIFESTO called the "Declaration of Sentiments" which boldly declared that "all men and women are created equal." The MANIFESTO launched the modern women's rights movement.

MANIFESTOS are not limited to the past or to political issues. In the early 1990's, IBM seemed OBLIVIOUS (Word 361) to the coming Internet revolution. Determined to wake the corporate giant up, David Grossman wrote a "Get Connected Manifesto" calling upon IBM to catch the Internet wave. Grossman's MANIFESTO worked and IBM is now an e-business powerhouse.

236. ENFRANCHISE:
To receive the right to vote

DISENFRANCHISE:
To lose the right to vote

In American history, Jim Crow laws DISENFRAN-CHISED African-American voters while the Voting Rights Act of 1965 ENFRANCHISED African-American voters. Ratified in 1920, the Nineteenth Amendment ENFRANCHISED millions of American women. The Twenty-sixth Amendment ENFRANCHISED eighteen-year-old American citizens.

237. COERCE:
To force to act or think in a certain way by use of pressure, threats or torture; compel

When the movie "Iron Man" opens, Tony Stark is on a business trip to Afghanistan to demonstrate Stark Industries' powerful new weapon, the "Jericho" cluster missile. Following a successful display of the Jericho's awesome destructive power, Stark's convoy is suddenly attacked by a terrorist group called the Ten Rings. The terrorists capture Stark and demand that he build a Jericho missile for them. When he refuses, the terrorists torture Stark in a FUTILE (Word 46) attempt to COERCE him into constructing the deadly weapon. After these tactics fail, the terrorists successfully COERCE Stark into ACQUIESCING (Word 43) by threatening to kill his fellow captive, Dr. Yinsen. Instead, Stark and Yinsen outsmart the terrorists by building a crude but strong suit of power armor enabling Stark to overpower his captors and escape.

238. EGALITARIAN:

Favoring social equality; belief in a society in which all people have equal political, economic, and civil rights

During the nineteenth century, American utopian leaders were inspired by a dream of creating EGALITARIAN communities. Founded by John Humphrey Noyes, the Oneida Community in upstate New York became a flourishing EGALITARIAN commonwealth of some 300 people. Men and women shared equally in all the community's tasks, from field to factory to kitchen. The members lived in one building and ate in a common dining hall.

The dream of EGALITARIAN living did not last. The communal dining hall ultimately became a restaurant where meals were bought with money. Led by Noyes's son, Pierrepont, Oneida Community, Ltd., grew into the world's leading manufacturer of stainless steel knives, forks and spoons with annual sales of half-a billion dollars.

239. BELLIGERENT:

Hostile and aggressive; warlike

When the movie "Braveheart" opens, Scotland is suffering under the cruel and AUTOCRATIC (see Word 234) rule of the English King Edward I. Hoping to avoid politics, William Wallace tries to live as a simple farmer. But Wallace is drawn into the struggle for freedom when an English magistrate brutally kills his wife, Murron. Enraged, Wallace vows revenge and is transformed into the BELLIGERENT leader of the Scottish rebels.

240. INQUISITION:

A severe interrogation; a systematic questioning

The INQUISITION was a formal court of justice established by the Roman Catholic Church (1232-1820) to discover and suppress HERESY (false beliefs). Although the United States has never had a formal court of INQUISITION, numerous zealots have conducted INQUISITIONS into the conduct of public officials. The best known of these INQUISITIONS was conducted by Senator McCarthy during the early 1950's. McCarthy ruthlessly questioned public officials as part of his campaign against alleged Communists.

241. AMELIORATE:

To make a situation better

EXACERBATE

To make a situation worse

What do Dorothea Dix, Ida B. Wells-Barnett and Batman have in common? All three were crusaders who dedicated themselves to AMELIORATING social problems. Dorothea Dix worked to AMELIORATE the lives of the INDIGENT (Word 221) insane by creating the first generation of American mental hospitals. Ida B. Wells-Barnett worked to AMELIORATE the lives of African Americans by exposing the problem of lynching in the South. And Batman worked to AMELIORATE the lives of the citizens of Gotham City by fighting the power of its crime bosses.

While all three of these crusaders succeeded in AMELIORATING social problems, Batman learned PARADOXICALLY (Word 41) that his efforts also EXACERBATED Gotham's crime problem by leading to an escalation of violence. At the end of "Batman Begins," Lieutenant Gordon warned Batman that when "we start carrying semi-automatics, they buy automatics. We start wearing Kevlar, they buy armor-piercing rounds." Lieutenant Gordon's DISQUIETING (Word 337) warning proved to be PRESCIENT (Word 340) as the Joker's arrival EXACERBATED Gotham's crime problem.

242. CONTIGUOUS:
Sharing an edge or boundary; touching

Which of the following is the southernmost city in the 48 CONTIGUOUS states?

(A) Kaalaulu, Hawaii
(B) Key West, Florida

The answer depends upon the meaning of the word CONTIGUOUS. Since the 48 CONTIGUOUS or touching states do not include Hawaii (or Alaska), the correct answer is B. Hawaii is actually an ARCHIPELAGO (chain of islands) located in the central Pacific Ocean about 2,000 miles southwest of the 48 CONTIGUOUS states. Kaalaulu is the southernmost city in the 50 states.

243. DESICCATE:
Thoroughly dried out; lifeless, totally arid

Antarctica is technically a desert that receives less than two inches of precipitation a year. One interior region of the Antarctic is known as the Dry Valleys. These valleys have not seen rainfall in over two million years. The Dry Valleys exist because 100 mph Katabatic down winds DESICCATE all moisture. The freezing temperatures and the absence of water and all life simulate conditions on the Planet Mars. As a result, the region is used as a training ground for astronauts who may one day make a voyage to the equally DESICCATED Red Planet.

D. LAW AND ORDER: THESE WORDS WILL HELP YOU UNDERSTAND HOW THE WHEELS OF JUSTICE TURN

244. PERTINENT:
Relevant; to the point; a clear illustration of a major point

In the movie, "Remember the Titans," Gerry criticizes Julius for not listening to his coaches and for selfish play that lets his teammates down. Julius defends himself by asking Gerry these PERTINENT questions: "Why should I give a hoot about you or anybody else out there? You are the Captain, right? Then why don't you tell your white buddies to block for Rev or Plugged Nickel? I'm supposed to wear myself out for the team. What team?" When Gerry reacts by saying "that's the worst attitude I ever heard," Julius responds with this PERTINENT point: "Attitude reflects leadership, Captain."

245. COMPLICITY:
Association or participation in a wrongful act

Tupac Shakur is widely believed to be America's greatest and most successful rapper with 75 million albums sold worldwide and over 50 million in the United States. On September 7, 1996, Shakur was shot four times in a drive-by shooting in Las Vegas. He died six days later. Because of their bitter rivalry with Tupac, rappers Biggie Smalls and Sean Combs were suspected of COMPLICITY in the murder. However, both Biggie and Combs vigorously denied any COMPLICITY in Tupac's death. Despite many investigations, the case remains unsolved.

246. EXONERATE and EXCULPATE:
Both mean to free from guilt or blame

What do Benjamin Franklin Gates ("National Treasure: Book of Secrets") and Harry Potter have in common? They both EXONERATED members of their families of EXECRABLE (Word 339) crimes. Ben successfully EXCULPATED his great-great grandfather, Thomas Gates of COMPLICITY (Word 245) in the plot to assassinate Abraham Lincoln. Harry successfully EXONERATED his godfather Sirius Black of the murder of Peter Pettigrew and 12 Muggles.

247. INDISPUTABLE:
Not open to question; undeniable; irrefutable

Who killed President Kennedy? The Warren Commission published a comprehensive report providing what it believed was INDISPUTABLE evidence that Lee Harvey Oswald acted alone. However, SKEPTICS (Word 102) soon criticized the Warren Commission's findings. In the movie "JFK," director Oliver Stone presents what he considers INDISPUTABLE evidence that Lee Harvey Oswald was in fact part of a secret conspiracy to kill President Kennedy.

248. PRECEDENT:

An act or instance that may be used as an example in dealing with subsequent similar instances

Suppose you were part of a group scheduled to visit the White House and meet the President. How would you address the President and upon meeting him (or her) what would you do? These issues have been settled by long-established PRECEDENTS. Washington rejected "His Highness" and "His High Mightiness" for the simple greeting "Mr. President." After saying "Mr. President, it is an honor to meet you," would you bow or shake hands? Although Washington favored bowing, Thomas Jefferson felt the practice was too royal. Feeling that this gesture was more democratic, he established the PRECEDENT of shaking hands.

249. UNPRECEDENTED:

Without previous example; an UNPRECEDENTED event has never happened before.

What do Tiger Woods and Will Smith have in common? Both have achieved UNPRECEDENTED success in their careers. Tiger Woods is on course to become the first billionaire athlete. It is interesting to note that prize money only accounts for about one-tenth of Tiger's earnings with the rest coming from LUCRATIVE (Word 217) endorsements. Like Tiger, Will Smith has achieved UNPRECEDENTED success. As a result of the popularity of "Hancock," Smith now has a streak of eight consecutive movies that have grossed over $100 million in ticket sales. This UNPRECEDENTED achievement establishes Will Smith as Hollywood's most marketable movie star.

250. MALFEASANCE:

Misconduct or wrongdoing especially by a public official

In just 15 years, Enron grew from an unknown company to become America's seventh largest corporation, employing 21,000 staff in more than 40 countries. But the firm's success turned out to have involved widespread MALFEASANCE including fraud, concealing debts and shredding documents. When its MALFEASANCE was finally revealed, Enron's stock plummeted from over $90.00 a share to less than 50 cents.

Testing Your Vocabulary

Each SAT contains 19 sentence completion questions that are primarily a test of your vocabulary. Each sentence completion will always have a key word or phrase that will lead you to the correct answer. Use the vocabulary from Chapters 6-7 to circle the answer to each of the following 10 sentence completion questions. You'll find answers and explanations on pages 50 -51.

1. Museum officials hailed the patron's gift as both _____ and _____: it was very generous and without previous example.

    (A) ironic .. pertinent
    (B) munificent .. unprecedented
    (C) extravagant .. egalitarian
    (D) parsimonious .. enlightened
    (E) belligerent .. empirical

2. The new labor contract was reached by _____ and compromise, not by force and _____.

    (A) allusion .. hyperbole
    (B) malfeasance .. manifesto
    (C) avarice .. disenfranchisement
    (D) consensus .. coercion
    (E) osmosis .. appeasement

3. The revolutionary leaders produced _____ that both clearly and succinctly declared their major beliefs while calling upon their followers to rise up against their oppressors.

   (A) a memoir
   (B) a manifesto
   (C) a caricature
   (D) a pretext
   (E) an anecdote

4. The forceful personality and generous patronage of Pope Julius II acted as _____, triggering an outpouring of artistic creativity now known as the High Renaissance.

   (A) a pretext
   (B) a metaphor
   (C) a catalyst
   (D) an allusion
   (E) an accord

5. Approved in 1920, the Nineteenth Amendment _____ millions of American women who had been denied the right to vote since the ratification of the Constitution in 1789.

   (A) enfranchised
   (B) depreciated
   (C) remunerated
   (D) enlightened
   (E) nullified

6. The storming of the Bastille on July 14, 1789 represents _____ event in French history, forever marking the end of the ancient regime and the beginning of a new democratic order.

    (A) an ironic
    (B) an empirical
    (C) a contiguous
    (D) a synthetic
    (E) a watershed

7. Shilpa's _____ was the antithesis of her brother's generosity: she was very greedy, while he was very _____.

    (A) destitution .. affluence
    (B) irrelevance .. pertinent
    (C) inquisitiveness .. indifferent
    (D) egalitarianism .. autocratic
    (E) avarice .. munificent

8. The mayor's chief of staff successfully cleared herself of charges of _____ by proving that a member of the town council had clandestinely misappropriated the missing funds.

    (A) belligerence
    (B) appeasement
    (C) malfeasance
    (D) destitution
    (E) caricature

9. Critics justifiably charged that Getlein's _____ leanings would eventually undermine the company's _____ culture that had always prized an open and nonhierarchical structure.

   (A) entrepreneurial .. creative
   (B) parsimonious .. inquisitive
   (C) empirical .. enlightened
   (D) sedentary .. consensus
   (E) autocratic .. egalitarian

10. Initially confined to a remote mountain village, the disease proved to be remarkably _____ as it infected people throughout the entire country.

   (A) virulent
   (B) synthetic
   (C) sedentary
   (D) caustic
   (E) complicitous

Answers and Explanations

1. **B**

   The question asks you to find a first word that means "very generous" and a second word that means "without previous example." The correct answer is MUNIFICENT (Word 222) and UNPRECEDENTED (Word 249).

2. **D**

   The question asks you to find a first word that is consistent with "compromise" and a second word that is consistent with "force." Since compromise and force are antonyms the answer must also be a pair of antonyms. The correct answer is CONSENSUS (Word 233) and COERCION (Word 237).

3. **B**

   The question asks you to find a word describing a public declaration of beliefs. The correct answer is MANIFESTO (Word 235).

4. **C**

   The question asks you to find a word means "triggering." The correct answer is CATALYST (Word 206).

5. **A**

   The question asks you to find a word that describes the process by which people gain the right to vote. The correct answer is ENFRANCHISED (Word 236).

6. E

The question asks you to find a word that describes a pivotal or turning point event. The correct answer is WATERSHED (Word 232).

7. E

The question asks you to find a first word that means "very greedy" and a second word that means "generosity." The key word "antithesis" or opposite signals that the answer will be a pair of antonyms. The correct answer is AVARICE (Word 219) and MUNIFICENT (Word 222).

8. C

The question asks you to find a word that describes the misappropriation of funds. The correct answer is MALFEASANCE (Word 250).

9. E

The question asks you to find a first word that would have a negative impact upon the second word. The second word must be consistent with an organization that has an "open and nonhierarchical structure." The correct answer is AUTOCRATIC (Word 234) and EGALITARIAN (Word 238) because Getlein's AUTOCRATIC leanings would mean that he would want more and more power and would thus "undermine" the company's egalitarian culture.

10. A

The question asks you to find a word describing an "infectious" disease that quickly spread "throughout the entire country." The correct answer is VIRULENT (Word 211).

Chapter 8

WORDS WITH MULTIPLE MEANINGS: 251–265

Learning new vocabulary words is a challenge when a word has a single meaning. Many students are surprised to discover that there are words that have multiple meanings. For example, everyone knows that a flag is a rectangular piece of fabric with a distinctive design that is used to symbolize a nation. But FLAG can also mean to lose energy or interest.

SAT test writers have long been aware of words with multiple meanings. Since students think they know what these words mean they often eliminate the word and miss the question. In fact, words like FLAG are among the most missed words on the SAT.

This chapter will examine and illustrate 15 commonly used words with multiple meanings. Our focus will be on these words' secondary definitions, the ones SAT test writers use to test your knowledge. So be prepared to learn that everyday words like CHECK, COIN and even GRAVITY have less commonly used secondary meanings.

251. ARREST:

To bring to a stop; halt

What is the first thing you think of when you hear the word ARREST? For most people, the word ARREST probably calls to mind a police officer and handcuffs. Arrest does mean to seize and hold under the authority of the law.

It is important to know that the word ARREST has other meanings. SAT test writers will use ARREST to mean to bring to a stop or halt. Environmentalists, for example, hope to ARREST the growth of carbon dioxide emissions into the earth's atmosphere. One way to remember this use of ARREST is to think of a cardiac ARREST. This condition takes place when there is an abrupt stoppage of normal blood circulation due to heart failure.

252. GRAVITY:

A serious situation or problem

Everyone has heard the expression, "Whatever goes up, must come down." This saying is true because of the law of gravity. In physics, gravity refers to the natural force of attraction exerted by a celestial body.

On the SAT, GRAVITY refers to a serious situation or problem. For example, on the television program "Grey's Anatomy," when Dr. Isobel "Izzie" Stevens was just 16, she gave birth to a daughter whom she gave up for adoption. Now 11 years old and sick with leukemia, Hannah desperately needs an immediate bone marrow transplant. Recognizing the GRAVITY of the situation, Izzie agrees to donate the bone marrow to save the daughter she never knew.

253. PRECIPITATE:
A result or outcome of an action

Most people associate the word PRECIPITATE with rain, mist, snow or sleet. However, PRECIPITATE can also refer to a result or outcome of an action. Test writers frequently use PRECIPITATE on AP US History questions. For example, the Cuban Missile Crisis was PRECIPITATED by the discovery of Soviet missiles in Cuba.

254. RELIEF:
Elevation of a land surface

What is the first thing that comes to your mind when you hear the word RELIEF? In everyday usage, RELIEF most commonly refers to the feeling of ease when a burden has been removed or lightened. For example, in baseball a RELIEF pitcher eases the burden of the starting pitcher. However, RELIEF can also be used as a geographic term that refers to the elevation of a land surface. For example, RELIEF maps of the United States rise at the Appalachian Mountains in the East and at the Rocky Mountains in the West.

255. CHECK:
To restrain; halt; hold back; contain

We are all familiar with the word CHECK. We earn checks, cash checks and check our work on math problems. Airline passengers check in at the ticket counter and hotel guests check in at the registration counter. SAT test writers know that you are familiar with these everyday uses of the word CHECK. It is important to remember that the word CHECK can also mean to restrain, halt, or hold back. For example, our Constitution calls for a system of CHECKS and balances to restrain each branch of government. During the Cold War, the U.S. policy of containment was designed to CHECK the expansion of Soviet power and influence. And hockey fans know that a CHECK is when one player blocks or impedes the movement of an opponent.

256. FLAG:

To become weak, feeble, or spiritless; to lose interest

Like CHECK (Word 255), FLAG is a common word with which we are all familiar. For most people, a flag is a banner or emblem used to symbolize a country, state or community. FLAG, however, can also mean to become weak or to lose interest. Whenever the singer Beyoncé wins an award, for example, she always thanks her parents for keeping her spirits up and never letting her enthusiasm FLAG. She says that her parents keep her motivation strong and her mind focused.

257. DISCRIMINATING:

Characterized by the ability to make fine distinctions; refined taste

Is DISCRIMINATING a negative or a positive word? Surprisingly, it can be both. Most people consider DISCRIMINATING a negative word because it refers to the act of treating a person, racial group or minority unfairly. Surprisingly, DISCRIMINATING can be a positive word when it refers to someone's ability to make fine distinctions and thus demonstrate good taste. For example, CONNOISSEURS (knowledgeable amateurs) are known for their DISCRIMINATING taste in rare wine, fine clothes and valuable art. In the James Bond movies, Bond is a secret agent who displays DISCRIMINATING taste by ordering vodka martinis ("shaken, not stirred"), wearing Omega watches and wearing stylish tuxedos.

258. ECLIPSE:
Overshadow; outshine; surpass

In astronomy, an ECLIPSE is the total or partial covering of one celestial body by another. A solar ECLIPSE, for example, occurs when the moon passes between the sun and the earth. ECLIPSE, however, can also be a verb meaning to overshadow or surpass. Taylor Hicks, for instance, won the fifth season of "American Idol." The fourth place finisher, Chris Daughtry nonetheless ECLIPSED Hicks in both popularity and record sales. A similar pattern can be seen in IndyCar racing. Scott Dixon won the 2008 Indianapolis 500. Although she didn't finish the race, Danica Patrick has ECLIPSED Dixon in both media attention and endorsements.

259. COIN:
To devise a new word or phrase

If you see the word COIN in a PSAT or SAT question, the first image that will probably come to your mind will be the image of a penny, nickel, dime or quarter.

While COIN is most commonly used to refer to a small piece of money, it can also mean to create a new word or phrase. The English language is not static. New words are COINED or created all the time. For example, Janine Benyus is a natural sciences writer who COINED the word "biomimicry" to describe the art of copying nature's biological principles of design. Ms. Benyus COINED the term by combining the Greek "bios," meaning "life," and "mimesis," meaning "imitate." For example, architects in London are using biomimetic principles derived from ocean sponges to design buildings that are far more energy efficient.

260. STOCK:
A stereotypical and formulaic character in a novel or film

The word STOCK has 13 different definitions ranging from the merchandise in a store to a unit of ownership in a company. While SAT test writers are aware of these different definitions, they are most interested in STOCK as a literary term referring to formulaic characters. Teen movies such as "Clueless," "Mean Girls" and "Superbad" all feature STOCK characters such as "The Perfect Girl," "The Blonde Bimbo," "The Popular Jock," and "The Awkward BUT Ultimately Beautiful Girl." These STOCK characters tend to be easily recognizable but one-dimensional and TRITE (Word 36).

261. CURRENCY:
General acceptance or use, prevalence

What is the first thought that comes to your mind when you hear the word CURRENCY? Most people probably immediately think of money. However, SAT test writers are not most people. They know that CURRENCY can also mean an idea that is becoming widespread or prevalent. For example, in his book *Quiet Strength*, Tony Dungy argues that a coach should treat his or her players with respect and avoid screaming at them. As Head Coach of the Indianapolis Colts, Dungy practices what he preaches. Although Dungy's view is gaining CURRENCY, many coaches still rely on old-fashioned TIRADES (Word 100) to motivate their players.

262. BENT:
A strong tendency; a leaning; an inclination

Have you ever said, "This nail is BENT, I can't use it?" For most people, the word BENT means twisted. However, BENT can also mean a strong tendency or disposition to follow a course of action. For example, the world famous artist Pablo Picasso demonstrated a BENT toward drawing from an early age. According to his family, Picasso's BENT was so great that he drew pictures before he could talk!

While Picasso's artistic BENT guided him to create works of art, the Joker's ("The Dark Knight") MALEVOLENT (malicious) BENT led him to create chaos and destruction. Because he is BENT on destruction for destruction's sake, the Joker is Batman's most formidable and IMPLACABLE (Word 182) foe.

263. COURT:

To attempt to gain the favor or support of a person or group

Most people associate the word COURT with a place. For example, a COURT is where people play tennis or basketball. A COURT is also a place where justice is administered by a judge or a jury. But, COURT can also be used as a verb. For example, when they run for office, politicians COURT votes. During the early 1970's, Richard Nixon COURTED the "Silent Majority," a group of voters who supported his Vietnam War policies and opposed the counterculture. In the 1980's, Ronald Reagan COURTED "Reagan Democrats," blue-collar workers who traditionally supported the Democratic party. Today, candidates from both parties are working hard to COURT young voters.

264. NEGOTIATE:

To successfully travel through, around or over an obstacle or terrain

The word NEGOTIATE is very familiar to students studying American history. Our national history is filled with examples of diplomats NEGOTIATING treaties and labor leaders NEGOTIATING contracts. But the word NEGOTIATE can also mean to successfully travel through, around or over an obstacle or difficult terrain. For example, settlers traveling along the Oregon Trail had to NEGOTIATE their way across broad streams and over steep mountain passes. In the Lord of the Rings trilogy, Frodo, Bilbo and Samwise had to NEGOTIATE a series of formidable obstacles before reaching the Crack of Doom in Mordor.

265. TEMPER:

To soften; moderate; MITIGATE (Word 31)

TEMPER is a word with contradictory meanings. On the one hand, TEMPER refers to a sudden burst of anger. On the other hand, TEMPER means to soften or moderate one's emotions. In the movie "Happy Gilmore," Happy illustrates both meanings of TEMPER. Happy loses his TEMPER on the golf course as he fights with Bob Barker and almost comes to blows with Shooter McGavin. Virginia successfully persuades Happy that he must TEMPER his anger. As a result, Happy defeats Shooter, wins over Virginia and saves his grandmother's home.

Testing Your Vocabulary

Each SAT contains 19 sentence completion questions that are primarily a test of your vocabulary. Each sentence completion will always have a key word or phrase that will lead you to the correct answer. Use the vocabulary from Chapters 6-8 to circle the answer to each of the following 10 sentence completion questions. You'll find answers and explanations on pages 66-68.

1. John Dean's accusations that top White House officials obstructed justice by trying to cover up the Watergate break-in _____ a sequence of events that led to President Nixon's resignation.

    (A) negotiated
    (B) precipitated
    (C) arrested
    (D) eclipsed
    (E) tempered

2. Determined to reduce global carbon dioxide emissions, leading environmentalists called for international _____ that _____ the growth of inefficient coal-burning factories.

    (A) paradigms .. foster
    (B) accords .. arrest
    (C) manifestos .. reaffirm
    (D) mandates .. encourage
    (E) anecdotes .. combat

3. The park guide warned the novice hikers to avoid advanced trails that contained rugged natural obstacles and were therefore difficult to _____.

    (A) court
    (B) eclipse
    (C) nullify
    (D) enfranchise
    (E) negotiate

4. Because they were based upon rigorously collected _____ data and not abstract theories, Professor Halle's revolutionary conclusions _____ all previous studies by making them obsolete.

    (A) experimental .. reinforced
    (B) stock .. surpassed
    (C) questionable .. strengthened
    (D) secondhand .. obliterated
    (E) empirical .. eclipsed

5. The once upbeat candidate had to _____ her initial optimism as new polling data indicated that her popular support had begun to significantly erode.

    (A) temper
    (B) coerce
    (C) intensify
    (D) exonerate
    (E) remunerate

6. Rapper Ludacris' name is actually an amalgam: he combined his given name Chris with the first part of the word ludicrous to _____ his popular stage name.

    (A) check
    (B) court
    (C) precipitate
    (D) coin
    (E) enlighten

7. Located in Australia, Uluru or Ayers Rock is an ancient sandstone formation that is often called an "island mountain" because it provides the only natural _____ in an otherwise flat and barren plain.

    (A) relief
    (B) bent
    (C) watershed
    (D) archipelago
    (E) paradigm

8. Americans understood the full _____ of the Cuban Missile Crisis when President Kennedy, calmly but with great seriousness, informed the public that any attack on the United States from Cuba would trigger a full nuclear retaliation against the Soviet Union.

    (A) currency
    (B) extravagance
    (C) virulence
    (D) gravity
    (E) avarice

9. Critics panned the new action adventure film saying that it was a trite story filled with _____ characters who were both formulaic and stereotypical.

    (A) munificent
    (B) unprecedented
    (C) stock
    (D) anecdotal
    (E) ironic

10. Selective taste and _____ judgment are essential for buying Modernist paintings, since a mistake can have expensive consequences.

    (A) belligerent
    (B) extravagant
    (C) synthetic
    (D) caustic
    (E) discriminating

Answers and Explanations

1. **B**

   The question asks you to find a word describing the impact of John Dean's accusations. The correct answer is PRECIPITATED (Word 253) since Dean's accusations led to President Nixon's resignation.

2. **B**

   The question asks you to find two logically connected actions that environmentalists committed to reducing global carbon dioxide emissions would advocate. The correct answer is ACCORDS (Word 226) and ARREST (Word 251). In other words, environmentalists want international agreements to halt the growth of carbon-burning factories.

3. **E**

   The question asks you to find a word describing the effect "rugged natural obstacles" would have on an advanced trail. The correct answer is NEGOTIATE (Word 264) since these obstacles would make the trail difficult to hike.

4. **E**

   The question asks you to find a first word that means "rigorously collected" and is the opposite of "abstract theories." The correct answer to the first blank is therefore EMPIRICAL (Word 212). The question then asks you to find a second word describing the impact Halle's EMPIR-ICALLY based revolutionary conclusions would have upon the previous theoretical studies. The correct answer to the second blank is ECLIPSED (Word 258) since the new EMPIRICAL data made all previous studies "obsolete."

5. **A**

The question asks you to find a word describing the impact the "new polling data" would have upon the "once-upbeat" candidate. The correct answer is TEMPER (WORD 265) since her falling popular support would force the candidate to TEMPER or moderate her "initial optimism."

6. **D**

The question asks you to find a word describing the creation of a new name or word. The correct answer is COIN (Word 259) since Ludacris is a coined or newly devised name.

7. **A**

The question asks you to find a word describing an "island mountain" on "an otherwise flat plain." The correct answer is RELIEF (Word 254) since Uluru or Ayers Rock is an elevated landform on a flat plain.

8. **D**

The question asks you to find a word that is consistent with President Kennedy's "great seriousness." The correct answer is GRAVITY (Word 252).

9. **C**

    The question asks you to find a word describing characters who "were both formulaic and stereotyped." The correct answer is STOCK (Word 260).

10. **E**

    The question asks you to find a word that is consistent with "selective taste" and logically essential to avoid making a mistake with "expensive consequences." The correct answer is DISCRIMINATING (Word 257).

Chapter 9

THE TOUGHEST WORDS I: 266–315

Do you know what the words DILATORY, CAPITULATE and BURGEON mean? If so, congratulations! You have an excellent vocabulary. If not, don't be upset. These words are all answers or answer choices to Level 5 questions, the toughest ones on the SAT. Only about 20 percent of students correctly answer a Level 5 question.

Paradoxically, Level 5 questions are both the toughest and the easiest on the SAT. They are tough because the word choices deliberately include challenging words known to only a small percentage of students. They are easy because if you know the words the clues are often very straightforward and lead directly to the correct answer.

Chapters 9 and 10 focus on 100 Level 5 vocabulary words. Each of these words was the answer to a very difficult question. Knowing the meaning of these words will significantly raise your SAT score by helping you infuse great vocabulary into your essay, understand difficult critical reading passages and master challenging sentence completion questions. As always, we have worked hard to find vivid examples to illustrate each word. Don't be DILATORY (late). There is no reason to CAPITULATE (surrender). Study these words and you will experience the pleasure of having a BURGEONING (rapidly expanding) vocabulary and a rising SAT score!

266. SCATHING:
Harshly critical

James Carville is a well known PUNDIT or commentator who offers his opinions on a variety of controversial topics. In an interview on Sports Center, Carville delivered this SCATHING criticism of the Bowl Championship Series (BCS): "The BCS is a stupid idea thought up by intellectual midgets trying to protect greedy college presidents."

267. QUIESCENT:
Marked by inactivity; a state of quiet repose

In A.D. 79, Pompeii was a prosperous Roman town of ten to twenty thousand people. Pompeians planted vineyards and grazed their sheep on the slopes of nearby Mt. Vesuvius. The mountain appeared to be benign and QUIESCENT, but looks can be deceiving. On August 24, A.D. 79, Mt. Vesuvius erupted, transforming Pompeii from a lively, crowded city into a ghost town. Modern geologists now know that Mt. Vesuvius is far from QUIESCENT. It is regarded as one of the most potentially dangerous volcanoes in the world because of the population of 3 million people who live close to it.

268. PROVISIONAL:
Tentative; temporary; for the time being (like a PROVISIONAL driver's license)

Quick: how many planets are there in the Solar System? If you answered 9 you were right up until 2006. From the time of its discovery in 1930 until 2006, Pluto was counted as the Solar System's 9th planet.

However, this classification proved to be PROVISION-AL. On August 24, 2006 the International Astronomical Union (IAU) reclassified Pluto as a member of a new category of dwarf planets. So now the Solar System contains 8 official planets and at least three dwarf planets, including Pluto. Pluto's PROVISIONAL status has raised a storm of controversy. Insisting that Pluto should still be a planet, traditionalists have protested the IAU's decision. The controversy has resulted in the COINING (Word 259) of a new verb "plutoed." Chosen as the 2006 Word of the Year, "to Pluto" means to demote or devalue someone or something.

269. LURID:
Sensational; shocking; ghastly

During the late 1890's, newspaper publishers led by William Randolph Hearst and Joseph Pulitzer attempted to outdo each other with sensational headlines and LURID stories about alleged atrocities in Cuba. For example, Hearst's Journal published a LURID sketch depicting Spanish officials disrobing and searching an American woman.

270. TRUCULENT and PUGNACIOUS:
Defiantly aggressive; eager to fight

On February 15, 1898, the battleship *Maine* mysteriously blew up with the loss of 200 sailors in Havana harbor. Led by Theodore Roosevelt, TRUCULENT Americans demanded that President McKinley call for a declaration of war. When the cautious president delayed, the PUGNACIOUS Roosevelt reportedly snarled that McKinley had "the back-bone of a chocolate éclair."

271. PROPITIATE:

To appease; conciliate; regain the favor or goodwill

Stung by Roosevelt's barb (see Word 270) and shaken by the public's demand for revenge, President McKinley recognized the inevitable and PROPITIATED both Roosevelt and the public. On April, 11, 1898, McKinley sent a war message to Congress urging armed intervention to avenge the sinking of the *Maine* and to free oppressed Cubans.

272. ÉLAN:

Vigorous spirit; great enthusiasm

A leader of unbounded energy, Theodore Roosevelt promptly formed a volunteer regiment nicknamed the "Rough Riders" to spearhead the American invasion of Cuba. The Rough Riders included a mixture of cowboys, Ivy League graduates and star athletes. Although short on discipline, the Rough Riders were long on ÉLAN. Dressed in a uniform custom-made by Brooks Brothers, TR demonstrated both courage and ÉLAN as he led a victorious charge up San Juan Hill.

273. PERFUNCTORY:

Something performed in a spiritless, mechanical and routine manner

In her "Shoop, Shoop Song," Cher famously poses this question: "Does he love me, I wanna know, how can I tell if he loves me so?" Cher provides the following answer: "If you wanna know if he loves you so, it's in his kiss, that's where it is." So what is the difference between a passionate kiss that proves he loves you and a PERFUNCTORY kiss that suggests he doesn't? A passionate kiss is filled with emotion and feeling. In contrast, a PERFUNCTORY kiss is a quick routine peck on the cheek. A PERFUNCTORY kiss probably means that a relationship is becoming routine and lacks passion.

274. APLOMB:
Self-assurance; confident composure; admirable poise under pressure

What do President Franklin D. Roosevelt and New York Giants quarterback Eli Manning have in common? Both demonstrated great APLOMB under enormous pressure. Faced with a deepening depression, Roosevelt calmed the nation by confidently proclaiming that, "the only thing we have to fear is fear itself." The President's APLOMB lifted the nation's spirit. Faced with his team trailing the undefeated New England Patriots by a score of 14 to 10, Eli Manning demonstrated impressive APLOMB as he led the Giants on an 83-yard winning drive during the final two minutes of Super Bowl LXII. We believe that learning the vocabulary words in this book will help you face the SAT with great APLOMB!

275. OPACITY:
Hard to understand; impenetrably dense and obscure

Read the sentence reprinted on the next page describing a painting entitled *October* by the modern American artist Kenneth Noland:

> *"The prototypical Circles, numbering some 175 examples, alone embrace a multitude of moods and means – from propulsive versus sundrenched hues to those of the type of October, displaying an economy, coolness, and quiddity that almost anticipate a Minimalist aesthetic."*

Do you understand what the author is trying to say? Is the writer LUCID (clear) or OPAQUE? If you were an editor would you keep or revise the sentence? Most editors would probably revise or delete this impenetrably dense sentence because its OPACITY makes it incomprehensible for all but the most knowledgeable readers.

276. CRAVEN:
Characterized by acting in a cowardly manner

What do Shaggy ("Scooby-Do") and the Cowardly Lion ("Wizard of Oz") have in common? Both are known for their CRAVEN behavior. Shaggy CRAVENLY cries "Zoinks!" whenever he is surprised or scared by suspected "monsters" and "ghosts." As everyone knows, the Cowardly Lion behaved in a CRAVEN manner because he lacked courage.

277. VENAL:
Corrupt, dishonest, open to bribery

What do the Ephors in the movie "300," and the NBA referee Tim Donaghy have in common? Both were VENAL officials. The Ephors were VENAL priests who betrayed the Spartans by accepting bribes from the Persians. Tim Donaghy was a VENAL NBA official who betrayed the players and their fans by betting on games that he officiated and by making calls that affected the point spread in those games.

278. LICENTIOUS:

Immoral; DISSOLUTE; debauched

Have you seen "300?" If so, you should have no trouble remembering the LICENTIOUS women in Xerxes' harem who successfully tempted Ephialtes. And in "Superbad," Seth, Evan, and Fogell all look forward to a LICENTIOUS evening at Jules' party.

279. NOXIOUS:

Harmful; injurious to physical; mental or moral health

China's lax environmental policies and repressive political system is NOXIOUS to its citizens' physical and moral well-being. Every night, columns of freight trucks spewing dark clouds of diesel exhaust rumble into China's crowded cities. These NOXIOUS fumes are by far China's largest source of street-level pollution. Meanwhile, China is a NOXIOUS one-party state where thousands of its citizens are imprisoned for "crimes" ranging from advocating a multiparty system to using the Internet to call for government reform.

280. SUPERFLUOUS:

Unnecessary; extra

The movie "The Dark Knight," includes scenes in which Batman leaves Gotham City and travels to Hong Kong. This marks the first time that Batman has ever left Gotham. While some critics and fans praised this UNPRECEDENTED (Word 249) dramatic development, others criticized it as a SUPERFLUOUS subplot. For example, one movie critic called it a "pointless jaunt" in an otherwise brilliant movie. What is your opinion? Do you think the Hong Kong scenes were essential to the story or were they a SUPERFLUOUS subplot that should have been deleted?

281. DUPLICITOUS:
Deliberate deceptiveness in behavior or speech

What do Ferris Bueller ("Ferris Bueller's Day Off") Dewey Finn ("School of Rock") and Frank Abagnale Jr. ("Catch Me if You Can") have in common? All three were DUPLICITOUS, but all three lied with great PANACHE (Word 81) or flair. Ferris dined at an expensive restaurant while pretending to be Abe Fromer, a Chicago sausage king. Dewey impersonated Ned so that he could take a job as a substitute teacher at a prestigious elementary school. And the 18-year-old Frank convinced Brenda that he was a Harvard graduate, a doctor and a Lutheran.

282. PROFLIGATE:
Wasteful, someone who SQUANDERS (wastes) time and money by living for the moment

Hollywood stars tend to be more PROFLIGATE than PARSIMONIOUS (Word 223). Tom and Katie Cruise's motto seems to be "Spend, spend, spend." Tom owns four private jets including a $28 million Gulfstream. The Cruises annually spend over $1 million just on fuel for their jaunts around the world. The PROFLIGATE couple recently spent $100,000 on a birthday party for their two-year-old daughter Suri. They filled a rented Hollywood Hills mansion with $17,000 worth of flowers and spent almost $5,000 on cakes. Each of the lucky guests received a personalized cake!

283. EPIPHANY:
A sudden realization, an insightful moment

The "Simpsons Movie" contains an excellent example of an EPIPHANY. While enjoying life in Alaska, the Simpsons see an advertisement presented by Tom Hanks promoting a new Grand Canyon to be located at the current site of Springfield. Marge and the kids decide that they must save Springfield. However, Homer is unconvinced. He refuses to help the town that tried to kill him. But then Homer visits a mysterious Inuit Shaman. Homer has a vision and suddenly has an EPIPHANY: he must save Springfield!

284. INSIDIOUS:
Causing harm in a subtle or stealthy manner; devious

In *The Scarlet Letter*, Roger Chillingworth is Hester Prynne's long-absent husband. He returns to Boston only to find that Hester has had an affair with an unknown man and is now the mother of an illegitimate daughter. Consumed with revenge, Chillingworth vows to find and then psychologically torture Hester's secret lover. Sensing a hidden guilt, Chillingworth soon launches an INSIDIOUS plan to torment the Reverend Arthur Dimmesdale.

285. VACUOUS:
Empty; lacking serious purpose

In the movie "Clueless," Josh accuses Cher of being VACUOUS by calling her a "SUPERFICIAL (shallow) space cadet" who lacks a serious purpose. At first, Cher denies being VACUOUS saying that she has donated many expensive Italian outfits to the family maid. Stung by Josh's criticism, Cher vows to give up her VACUOUS lifestyle and find a new more serious purpose.

286. HARBINGER, PORTENT, PRESAGE:
Both are indications or omens that something important or calamitous is about to occur

Recent scientific studies have confirmed that the North Pole is melting. This startling fact PRESAGES difficult times for polar bears and other Arctic animals that rely on sea ice to survive. It is also a HARBINGER of coming trouble for humans. The melting ice will raise sea levels thus posing a threat to coastal cities and villages. Alarmed scientists are warning world leaders that these PORTENTS should not be ignored. They are calling for international ACCORDS (Word 226) to ARREST (Word 251) the growth of carbon dioxide emissions.

287. BELEAGUER:
To beset; to surround with problems

In the movie, "Remember the Titans," Herman Boone, a successful black football coach from North Carolina, is hired to replace the popular white coach Bill Yoast at newly integrated T.C. Williams High School in

Alexandria, Virginia. Boone is immediately BELEAG-UERED by a host of problems. Outraged by his demotion, Yoast threatens to resign. At the same time, tensions quickly erupt between black and white members of the football team. These tensions reflect the turmoil in Alexandria, where extremists resent Coach Boone and demand that he resign.

288. BURGEON:
To rapidly grow and expand

Although BELEAGUERED (see Word 287) by seemingly INSURMOUNTABLE (Word 185) problems, Coach Boone proved to be RESOLUTE (Word 315) and resourceful. He ADROITLY (Word 67) unified both his coaching staff and his team. Once they learned to work together, the Titans won victory after victory. Community support soon BURGEONED as the town and school rallied behind their victorious and unified football team.

289. IMPERIOUS:
Domineering and arrogant; haughty

What do the Persian ruler Xerxes, the English King Henry VIII and the French king Louis XIV have in common? All three were IMPERIOUS leaders. Xerxes IMPERIOUSLY insisted that his subjects all bow down before their god-king. Henry VIII IMPERIOUS-LY demanded obedience from his subjects and from his wives. Louis XIV IMPERIOUSLY (but truthfully) explained that in France, "L'etat, c'est moi," meaning "the state is me."

290. PETULANT:
Peevish, irritable

Britney Spears is notorious for her PETULANT behavior. For example, just an hour before going on stage at the MTV Video Music Awards, Britney PETULANTLY insisted on doing her own hair. She abruptly told her hair stylist, "You're really annoying me. Get out!" The PETULANT Pop Princess ended up doing her own hair which proved to be a FIASCO (Word 146).

291. COMPLAISANT and AFFABLE:
Both mean amiable; agreeable; marked by a pleasing personality

Compare Britney Spears with Giselle, the fairy tale princess, in the movie "Enchanted." While Britney is PETULANT (Word 290) and peevish, Giselle exudes a natural goodness that delights both humans and animals. Her COMPLAISANT personality even charms notoriously ill-tempered New Yorkers who stop what they are doing to spontaneously sing and dance with the ever AFFABLE Giselle.

It is important to note that although COMPLAISANT and complacent sound alike, they are two very different words. Complacent means over contented and self-satisfied. In contrast, COMPLAISANT is derived from the prefix *com* meaning "with" and the root *plaisir* meaning "pleasure." So COMPLAISANT literally means "with pleasure" and thus demonstrating a pleasing personality.

292. FAWN:

To behave in a servile manner; subservient

In "300" Xerxes promises Leonidas great wealth and power. All the Spartan king has to do is kneel before the Persian god-king. But Leonidas is a proud Spartan who refuses to act in a FAWNING manner toward anyone. Leonidas rebuffs Xerxes saying, "kneeling will be hard for me. I'm afraid killing all those slaves of yours has left me with a nasty cramp in my leg."

293. OBDURATE:

Very stubborn; obstinate; unyieldingly persistent; inflexible; INTRACTABLE

What do the Spartan leader King Leonidas and President Woodrow Wilson have in common? They were both very OBDURATE. In the movie "300," Leonidas OBDURATELY insisted that "the battle is over when I say it is over. No surrender. No retreat." Similarly, Wilson OBDURATELY refused to accept any of Senator Lodge's reservations that would modify the League of Nations. "I shall consent to nothing," Wilson OBDURATELY insisted.

294. REDOLENT:

Exuding fragrance; full of a specified smell

In her Harry Potter series, author J.K. Rowling often describes how the REDOLENT fragrance of a particularly delicious feast would WAFT (float) across the Great Hall at Hogwarts.

In Faulkner's novels, the REDOLENT fragrance of magnolia blooms seems almost to WAFT from the book's pages.

295. CHICANERY:

Deception by artful subterfuge; deliberate trickery

In her book, *Century of Dishonor*, Helen Hunt Jackson exposed the American government's CHICANERY in deliberately cheating the Native Americans. For example, Jackson sharply criticized government officials for their CHICANERY in signing treaties they had no intention of honoring.

In the movie "Iron Man," Pepper Potts exposed Obadiah Stane's CHICANERY in deliberately selling weapons to both the U.S. troops and the Ten Rings terrorists. Stane's CHICANERY did not end with supplying weapons to American's enemies. Potts discovered that Stane also hired the terrorists to kill his business partner Tony Stark.

296. CONUNDRUM:

A difficult problem; a dilemma with no easy solution

In the movie "Knocked Up," slacker Ben Stone and ambitious career-minded Allison Scott meet at a local night club and then spend the night together. The following morning, they quickly discover that they have little in common. Eight weeks later, Allison is shocked to discover that she is pregnant. She then contacts the equally shocked Ben to tell him the news. Allison and Ben now face a difficult CONUNDRUM. Will Allison choose to be a single mother or will she and Ben give their relationship a chance?

297. SLIGHT:

A disrespectful, disparaging remark; a put down

In Volume 1, Grand Master Larry DEBUNKED (Word 178) Britney Spears' ex-husband Kevin Federline. Now it's Britney's turn to face GML's razor-sharp SLIGHTS, SAGE (wise) advice and PERTINENT (Word 244) questions:

> *Yo Britney you're easy to SLIGHT,*
> *Cause we're not tight.*
> *I don't want to frighten,*
> *I'm here to ENLIGHTEN (Word 227).*
>
> *Once your fans were ELATED (very happy),*
> *Your songs were gold-plated.*
> *Now they rejoice,*
> *When they don't hear your voice.*
>
> *Being BOORISH (Word 64) is not refined,*
> *The way to success is clearly defined.*
> *Don't be so dumb,*
> *Act with more APLOMB (Word 274).*
>
> *It's time to take stock,*
> *Can you still rock?*
> *Are you still it?*
> *Or is it time to quit?*

298. CAPITULATE:

To surrender; comply without protest

What do the King Leonidas and General George Washington have in common? Both refused to CAPIT- ULATE when faced with certain defeat. In the movie

"300," King Leonidas refused to CAPITULATE to the Persians when he defiantly insisted, "Spartans never surrender. Spartans never retreat." Similarly, George Washington refused to CAPITULATE when the British and Hessians had apparently trapped his army on the Pennsylvania side of the Delaware River. Defiantly telling his troops, "Victory or Death!" Washington boldly crossed the ice-filled Delaware on Christmas eve and surprised the Hessians at Trenton.

299. DISHEARTENING:
Very discouraged; dismayed; dispirited

What do Samuel Tilden and Al Gore have in common? Both men were Democratic presidential candidates who won the popular vote but suffered DISHEART-ENING defeats in the Electoral College. Tilden lost the controversial 1876 election and Gore lost the hotly disputed 2000 election. However, both men overcame their DISHEARTENING defeats. Tilden became a major benefactor of the New York Public Library, and Gore has become one of the world's foremost environmental activists.

300. APOCRYPHAL:
Of doubtful authenticity; SPURIOUS (false)

What do the Spanish explorer Ponce de Leon and the English physicist Sir Isaac Newton have in common? Both are widely associated with APOCRYPHAL stories that did not happen. American students have long been taught that Ponce de Leon discovered Florida while searching for the Fountain of Youth. The story is APOCRYPHAL. While Ponce de Leon did discover Florida, there is no evidence that he was searching for a Fountain of Youth. Students have also been taught that Sir Isaac Newton was inspired to discover the laws of gravity when he was hit on the head by a falling apple. The story is APOCRYPHAL. While Newton did formulate laws of motion and gravitation there is no evidence that these laws came to him when he was sitting under an apple tree and struck by a falling piece of fruit.

301. MAGISTERIAL:
Learned and authoritative

In England, a magistrate was a royal official entrusted with the administration of the laws. Magistrates naturally wanted to appear MAGISTERIAL or learned and authoritative. In the movie, "The Wizard of Oz," the Munchkin mayor wanted to appear MAGISTERIAL when he grandly welcomed Dorothy by publicly proclaiming, "As Mayor of the Munchkin City in the County of the Land of Oz, I welcome you most regally." The Mayor's MAGISTERIAL tone continued when he announced that the Wicked Witch is "positively, absolutely, undeniably and reliably dead."

302. PLASTICITY, MALLEABLE, PLIABLE:
Flexible; easily shaped, especially by outside influences or forces

The 17th Century English philosopher John Locke argued that at birth the human mind is a blank tablet (a tabula rasa) and that as a result all of our ideas are shaped by experience. Locke thus believed that humans are by nature MALLEABLE. Modern public relations specialists have extended Locke's view to include the belief that public opinion is highly

PLASTIC and can thus be shaped. For example, in the movie "Hancock," Hancock is a SURLY (Word 336) superhero who is so disliked that most people in Los Angeles want him to leave their city. However, Ray Embrey is a public relations specialist who is determined to transform Hancock's image. Embrey's faith in the PLASTICITY of public opinion proves to be justified. Popular attitudes prove to be PLIABLE, and after he saves a policeman's life Hancock becomes a popular hero.

303. CHAGRIN:
The feeling of distress caused by humiliation, failure or embarrassment

In the movie "Anchorman," Brian Fantana is CHAGRINED when he discovers that his cologne is so foul smelling that it repels Veronica and everyone else in the newsroom.

In the movie "Pretty Woman," Vivian is deeply CHAGRINED when SUPERCILIOUS (Word 345) clerks in a fashionable clothing store refuse to help her because of the way she is dressed.

304. OBSTREPEROUS:
Noisily and stubbornly defiant; unruly; boisterous

The television program "Supernanny" features Jo Frost's amazing ability to tame even the wildest and most OBSTREPEROUS children. If you watch "Desperate Housewives," you know that Lynette and her husband could use help from the Supernanny to discipline their four OBSTREPEROUS children.

305. IDYLLIC:
Charmingly simple and carefree

What do Happy Land in "Happy Gilmore" and Andalasia in "Enchanted" have in common? Both are charming IDYLLIC places. Happy Land is an imaginary place where Happy can relax with Virginia and forget about Shooter McGavin. Andalasia is an IDYLLIC paradise where magical creatures and humans all live carefree blissful lives.

306. DILAPIDATED:
Having fallen into a state of disrepair; broken-down; in deplorable condition

In his autobiography *Black Boy*, Richard Wright provides a vivid description of the nightmare of living in a DILAPIDATED home furnished with broken furniture and filthy kitchen appliances. President Johnson's Great Society included urban renewal projects designed to rebuild DILAPIDATED neighborhoods like the ones Richard Wright lived in.

307. EXTEMPORIZE and IMPROVISE:
Both mean to lecture or speak without notes

What do Al Jolson ("The Jazz Singer"), Dr. Martin Luther King Jr., ("I Have a Dream"), and Dewey Finn ("School of Rock") have in common? All three EXTEMPORIZED at a critical moment in their careers. Al Jolson starred in "The Jazz Singer," the first talking movie. His first IMPROVISED words were: "Wait a minute! Wait a minute! You ain't heard nothin' yet!" Most people are unaware of the fact that Dr. King EXTEMPORIZED much of his famous "I Have a Dream" speech. And in "School of Rock," Dewey IMPROVISED a great math lesson when his principal unexpectedly entered his classroom.

308. MYRIAD:
Many; numerous

The United States now faces a MYRIAD of pressing problems including health care reform, global warming and the war on terrorism. While acknowledging that these problems are important, the billionaire Texas oilman and PHILANTHROPIST (Word 129) T. Boone Pickens believes that America's dependence upon expensive, imported oil poses our nation's most urgent problem. Pickens list of alternatives to oil includes coal, natural gas, bio fuels, solar power and wind energy. Pickens believes that while there are MYRIAD choices, wind energy is America's most VIABLE (Word 87) option. He points out that America is blessed with an extensive wind corridor that stretches in a north-south line across the nation's Great Plains. However, there is no national CONSENSUS (Word 233) as to whether this is the right solution or only a STOPGAP (Word 333) in dealing with our energy problems.

309. UNGAINLY:
Awkward; clumsy

What do Mia Thermopolis ("Princess Diaries") and Betty Suarez ("Ugly Betty") have in common? Both are AFFABLE (Word 291) but UNGAINLY young women. Mia is the fifteen-year-old heir to the throne of the fictional kingdom of Genovia. She attends an exclusive private school and is regularly teased by her peers for her UNGAINLY manners and frizzy hair. Betty works at the ultra chic New York City fashion magazine *Mode*. She is good-hearted but her thick-framed glasses and prominent set of extra-large dental braces underscore her UNGAINLY appearance.

310. DILATORY:
Habitually late; tardy

I'm here to inspire,
Now is not the time to tire.
You're doing fine,
It's near the end of Chapter Nine.

DILATORY means late,
So control your own fate.
Don't delay,
Study our words each day!

Grand Master Larry is right. Don't be DILATORY! Remember Emperor Charlemagne in Word 209? His strategy of trying to learn words by OSMOSIS proved to be FUTILE (Word 46). A more effective approach is to study a few words every day. Repetition is important. You might go to the Fast Review at the end of this volume and put a check beside each word you have learned. That will help mark your progress and let you know which words to concentrate more time on. Above all, don't be DILATORY! There are too many words to learn a few days before taking the test.

311. VITUPERATIVE and VITRIOLIC:
Characterized by verbal abuse; bitter criticism

Most critics panned Britney Spears' INEPT perform-ance at the VMA Awards Show. While some reviewers attempted to provide the former Pop Princess with constructive criticism, others wrote critiques that were astonishingly VITUPERATIVE. Here are some examples of their VITRIOLIC critique of Britney's performance:

- "Britney's wig, much like her talent, isn't real."

- "Zoned-out Britney was a flop."

- "How about the simple and final confirmation that she just can't sing."

312. DISCORDANT:

Not in harmony; incompatible; at variance with as in a DISCORDANT detail that doesn't fit a pattern

In *The Cornish Trilogy*, Francis Cornish is an art expert who specializes in finding DISCORDANT details to prove that a painting is not authentic. Cornish demonstrates his amazing powers of observation and command of ESOTERIC (Word 344) facts when he evaluates a painting thought to be by the 15th Century Dutch master Hubert van Eyck. The painting included a monkey hanging by its tail from the bars of Hell. This seemingly INNOCUOUS (Word 99) image proved to be a DISCORDANT detail. Monkeys with prehensile tails did not exist in Europe until the 16th Century. Since van Eyck died in 1426 the painting had to be a forgery!

313. PERFIDIOUS:

Treacherous; traitorous; deceitful

What do Judas Iscariot, Ephialtes, Benedict Arnold, and Peter Pettigrew have in common? All four were

PERFIDIOUS traitors and opportunists. Judas betrayed Christ, Ephialtes betrayed the 300 Spartans, Benedict Arnold betrayed the Colonial Army and Peter Pettigrew ("Wormtail") betrayed James and Lily Potter.

314. SUPINE:
Lying on one's back

Art historians believe that at least some of the Cro-Magnon cave artists may have painted the ceilings of low-lying caves from a SUPINE position. However, contrary to popular belief, Michelangelo did not paint the Sistine ceiling in a SUPINE position. He actually stood on a carefully constructed scaffold.

315. INDOMITABLE and RESOLUTE:
Very determined; unwavering

The Buffalo Bill's tight end Kevin Everett suffered a severe spinal cord injury while making a tackle in the opening game of the 2007 NFL season. Everett was paralyzed from the neck down when he arrived at Buffalo's Millard Fillmore Gates Hospital. Doctors initially feared that Everett would never walk again. But Everett remained RESOLUTE. State-of-the-art medical care and his own INDOMITABLE spirit gave Everett the will to fight every day for recovery. Remarkably, Everett is now able to walk again. His courage and RESOLUTE attitude have inspired others who have suffered similar injuries.

Testing Your Vocabulary

Each SAT contains 19 sentence completion questions that are primarily a test of your vocabulary. Each sentence completion will always have a key word or phrase that will lead you to the correct answer. Use the vocabulary from Chapters 6-9 to circle the answer to each of the following 10 sentence completion questions. You'll find answers and explanations on pages 95-96.

1.   The female subject of this painting by Henri Matisse seems _____, as if Matisse sought to portray an unconquerable female spirit.

    (A)   ungainly
    (B)   indomitable
    (C)   quiescent
    (D)   vacuous
    (E)   perfidious

2.   The coach urged his team's zealous fans to refrain from making any _____ remarks, ones that would be considered disrespectful or disparaging of the visiting team.

    (A)   perfunctory
    (B)   provisional
    (C)   contiguous
    (D)   anecdotal
    (E)   slighting

3. Some people alternate between contrasting temperaments; either they are _____ or they are _____.

    (A)   complaisant .. petulant
    (B)   indomitable .. resolute
    (C)   obdurate .. intractable
    (D)   imperious .. domineering
    (E)   truculent .. belligerent

4. Daniel Webster's reputation for sublime _____ was reinforced by his learned, authoritative and even _____ tone when delivering speeches on the Senate floor.

    (A)   comedy .. truculent
    (B)   diligence .. perfunctory
    (C)   oratory .. magisterial
    (D)   loyalty .. perfidious
    (E)   optimism .. disheartening

5. According to Suetonius, Roman society was _____ and dissolute, for _____ behavior was encouraged by the irresponsible aristocracy.

    (A)   gracious .. magisterial
    (B)   idyllic .. perfidious
    (C)   modest .. imperious
    (D)   debauched .. licentious
    (E)   duplicitous .. parsimonious

6. The salesman was known for both his _____ and his _____: he lied frequently but did so with great enthusiasm and flair.

    (A)   venality .. indifference
    (B)   pugnacity .. animation
    (C)   petulance .. aloofness
    (D)   complicity .. malfeasance
    (E)   duplicity .. élan

7. Linduff has an unquestionably _____ manner: she fawns on anyone who she perceives to be her superior.

    (A) imperious
    (B) inquisitive
    (C) discordant
    (D) belligerent
    (E) subservient

8. Although she was a capable student, Hannah typically engaged in _____ study habits by not preparing for her final exams until the last possible moment.

    (A) dilatory
    (B) superfluous
    (C) unprecedented
    (D) obstreperous
    (E) craven

9. Brianna was a friendly and conciliatory person; she had none of her brother's _____.

    (A) pugnacity
    (B) affability
    (C) venality
    (D) élan
    (E) extravagance

10. The now disgraced governor was _____ public official, who was corrupt and easily bribed.

    (A) a vituperative
    (B) an obdurate
    (C) a venal
    (D) an imperious
    (E) a craven

Answers and Explanations

1. **B**

    The question asks you to find a word that is consistent with the key phrase "unconquerable female spirit." The correct answer is INDOMITABLE (Word 315).

2. **E**

    The question asks you to find a word that is consistent with remarks that are "disrespectful and disparaging." The correct answer is SLIGHTING (Word 297).

3. **A**

    The question asks you to find a pair of answers that are opposites since the people "alternate between contrasting temperaments." The correct answer is COMPLAISANT (Word 291) and PETULANT (Word 290). All of the other answer choices were pairs of synonyms.

4. **C**

    The question asks you to find a first word that is consistent with "delivering speeches" and a second word that is consistent with being "learned and authoritative." The correct answer is ORATORY and MAGISTERIAL (Word 301).

5. **D**

    The question asks you to find a first word that is consistent with "dissolute" and a second word that describes a "dissolute" and "irresponsible" aristocracy. The correct answer is DEBAUCHED and LICENTIOUS (Word 278)

6. E

The question asks you to find a first word that means "lied frequently" and a second word that means "great enthusiasm and flair." The correct answer is DUPLICITY (Word 281) and ÉLAN (Word 272).

7. E

The question asks you to find a word that is consistent with the key word, "fawns." The correct answer is SUBSERVIENT (Word 292).

8. A

The question asks you to find a word that describes a student who waits "until the last possible moment" to study for final exams. The correct answer is DILATORY (Word 310).

9. A

The question asks you to find a word that means the opposite of "friendly and complaisant." The correct answer is PUGNACITY (Word 270).

10. C

The question asks you to find a word describing a "disgraced governor" who "was corrupt and easily bribed." The correct answer is VENAL (Word 277).

Chapter 10

THE TOUGHEST WORDS II: 316–365

Chapter 10 continues our goal of helping you learn the 100 toughest words on the SAT. As in Chapter 9, each of these words was the answer or answer choice to a Level 5 question. You'll find that we have used an ECLECTIC (variety) mix of popular and historic examples to help ELUCIDATE (clarify, explain) the meaning of each word. Our approach is always DIDACTIC (intended to instruct). Don't be CHURLISH (ill-tempered) or REFRACTORY (obstinate). Our SCINTILLATING (sparkling) examples will inspire you to complete the final 50 words. When you finish you'll be an articulate student who can write forcefully, speak eloquently and achieve soaring scores on the SAT!

316. IDIOSYNCRASY:
A trait or mannerism that is peculiar to an individual

Many of the most memorable movie villains have particularly vivid IDIOSYNCRASIES. For example, Austin Powers' archenemy Dr. Evil often bites the nail of his little finger. In the movie "The Dark Knight," Harvey "Two-Face" Dent is a schizophrenic DA-turned-villain who flips a coin before deciding whether to kill someone. If the victim makes the correct call, Two-Face will spare his or her life.

Villains are not the only film characters who have memorable IDIOSYNCRASIES. In the movie "Juno," Paulie has a PENCHANT (Word 62) for eating Tic Tacs. Juno is aware of this IDIOSYNCRASY and as a token of her love fills Paulie's mail box with boxes of Tic Tacs.

317. CENSORIOUS:
Highly critical

In the movie "Animal House," the Deltas are a group of BOORISH (Word 64) fraternity brothers who have done their best to provoke the CENSORIOUS Dean of Students, Vernon Wormer. Outraged by pranks which included filling trees with underwear and delivering medical school cadavers to an alumni dinner, Dean Wormer vows to revoke the Delta's charter and expel them from Faber College. Led by "Otter" and "Boon," the HEDONISTIC (Word 104) Deltas continue to infuriate their CENSORIOUS Dean and he puts the Deltas on "double secret probation." When the Deltas all fail their midterms, Dean Wormer expels them from school and happily notifies their draft boards of their eligibility. UNDAUNTED (Word 73), the Deltas seek revenge by wreaking havoc on Faber College's annual Homecoming parade.

318. CONSTERNATION:
A state of great dismay and confusion

In the movie "Juno," Juno MacGuff faces many difficult choices. After deciding against getting an abortion, Juno agrees to have a closed adoption with Vanessa and Mark Loring. The Lorings seem like the perfect couple because they are young and AFFLUENT (Word 221), and Vanessa has her heart set on becoming a mother. With everything seemingly agreed upon, Juno reacts with great CONSTER-NATION when Mark later tells her that he has decided to leave Vanessa. Juno ultimately overcomes her CONSTERNATION and stands by her agreement to give her baby to Vanessa.

319. DIDACTIC:
Designed or intended to teach and instruct

In the movie "Dead Poets Society," John Keating is a gifted but UNORTHODOX (Word 7) teacher at a strict private school. On the first day of class, Keating surprises his students by taking them on a "field trip" to look at former Welton students' photographs hanging in a trophy case. Keating points out that the boys in the old photographs had great dreams, "their eyes are full of hope, just like you." Keating's purpose is DIDACTIC. He wants to teach his students the idea of *carpe diem* (Latin for "seize the day") by emphasizing that time is fleeting and opportunities must be seized before it is too late.

320. ELUCIDATE:

To make clear or plain, especially by explanation

In the movie, "Dead Poets Society," John Keating (see Word 319) rejects the textbook's lifeless approach to poetry. Instead he ELUCIDATES an entirely different approach by explaining, "We don't read and write poetry because it's cute. We read and write poetry because we are members of the human race. And the race is filled with passion."

321. EFFUSIVE:

Unrestrained praise

Movie critics are normally restrained and hard-to-please. However, critics have been overwhelmingly EFFUSIVE in their praise for Christopher Nolan's work as the director of "The Dark Knight." Praising the film as "an EPIC (Word 198) masterpiece" and "quite possibly the best superhero movie ever made," critics have LAUDED (Word 91) Nolan for superbly crafted scenes that include innovative sequences shot using Imax cameras and breathtaking VERTIGINOUS (Word 343) mid-air escapes. Reviewers have not limited their EFFUSIVE praise to Nolan's DEFT (Word 67) cinematic techniques. They have also commended his ability to create complex characters who embody the moral AMBIGUITIES (Word 21) of a city where there is a constant tension between good and evil.

322. PROLIFIC:

Very productive

What do Kareem Abdul-Jabbar, Jerry Rice and Barry Bonds have in common? All three were professional athletes who were PROLIFIC scorers. Kareem Abdul-Jabbar was a PROLIFIC NBA center who scored a record 38,387 points. Jerry Rice was a PROLIFIC NFL receiver who scored a record 197 touchdowns. And Barry Bonds was a PROLIFIC MLB player who hit a record 762 home runs.

323. FUROR:

A general commotion; an uproar

What do Michael Jackson and Jamie Lynn Spears have in common? Both created a FUROR over their babies. On November 19, 2002, Michael Jackson shocked a crowd of fans by dangling his nine-month-old son over a balcony at his hotel in Berlin. The self-styled King of Pop's ill-considered action sparked a public FUROR that led to worldwide calls that the baby should be taken away by the Department of Social Services. Shaken by the FUROR, Jackson apologized admitting that he "made a terrible mistake," explaining that fans wanted to see his son.

Just five years later, Jamie Lynn Spears ignited a FUROR when the 16-year-old star of "Zoey 101" announced that she was 12 weeks pregnant. The announcement triggered a media frenzy and a public debate over teenage pregnancies. Polls showed that while a majority of Americans held Jamie Lynn responsible, 31 percent blamed her parents and 16 percent blamed her older sister Britney Spears.

324. PARANOIA:

A tendency on the part of an individual or group toward excessive or irrational suspiciousness; irrational fear

On February 9, 1950 Senator Joseph McCarthy (see Word 111) boldly announced to an audience in Wheeling, West Virginia, "I have here in my hand a list of 205 names known to the Secretary of State as being members of the Communist Party and who nevertheless are still working and shaping the policy of the State Department." Although the State Department later concluded that Senator McCarthy had perpetuated a "fraud and a hoax," no one was listening. Agitated by McCarthy's reckless charges, America entered a four-year period of PARANOIA and character assassination. Today, McCarthyism still refers to the PARANOIA created by sensational but unfounded allegations.

325. MARGINAL:

Of secondary importance; NOT central

Everyone agrees that Harry, Hermione, and Ron are central characters in the Harry Potter SAGA (Word 198). But can you identify Hannah Abbott? Probably not. Hannah was a MARGINAL character who was a member of Hufflepuff and Dumbledore's Army. As an adult she became the wife of Neville Longbottom and the land-lady of the Leaky Cauldron.

It is important to note that MARGINAL gives us the word MARGINALIZE. As you might guess, MARGINALIZE means to be relegated to a position of secondary importance.

326. OBFUSCATE:

To deliberately confuse; to make something so confusing that it is hard to understand

What do former Federal Reserve Chairman Alan Greenspan and the Gingerbread Man in "Shrek" have in common? Both knew how to OBFUSCATE in order avoid answering questions. Greenspan admitted that in order to avoid saying "no comment," he proceeded "with four or five sentences which become increasingly obscure. The Congress-person thinks I answered the question and goes onto the next one."

In the movie "Shrek," Lord Farquaad captured the Gingerbread Man and demanded to know who was hiding the remaining fairy-tale characters. But the valiant Gingerbread Man cleverly OBFUSCATED the truth:

> *Lord Farquaad:* Who is hiding them?
> *Gingerbread Man:* OK, I'll tell you. Do you know the Muffin Man?
> *Lord Farquaad:* The Muffin Man?
> *Gingerbread Man:* The Muffin Man!
> *Lord Farquaad:* Yes, I know the Muffin Man who lives on Drury Lane.
> *Gingerbread Man:* Well, she's married to the Muffin Man.
> *Lord Farquaad:* The Muffin Man?
> *Gingerbread Man:* The Muffin Man!
> *Lord Farquaad:* She's married to the Muffin Man!

327. FLUMMOX:
To confuse; perplex

What do viewers of the television series "Lost" and the movie series "Matrix" have in common? Both series have CONVOLUTED plots (see Word 75) that left many viewers FLUMMOXED. Viewers of "Lost" and "Matrix" were not the only ones left FLUMMOXED by the twists and turns of a complicated plot. The Gingerbread Man's clever OBFUSCATION (see Word 326) left Lord Farquaad FLUMMOXED.

328. SPATE:
A large number or amount

Each spring, fans of action adventure movies eagerly await the arrival of new blockbuster movies. Hollywood did not disappoint fans in the summer of 2008. Studios produced a SPATE of summer blockbusters, including "Iron Man," "The Dark Knight," "Hancock," "Wall-E" and "Indiana Jones and the Kingdom of the Crystal Skull."

329. INEFFABLE:
A feeling that cannot be put into words; indescribable

What do Josie ("Never Been Kissed") and Giselle ("Enchanted") have in common? Both experienced a special and thus INEFFABLE first kiss. Josie's IN-EFFABLE moment occurred when Mr. Coulson kissed her on the pitcher's mound in front of most of the student body. Giselle's INEFFABLE moment occurred when she shared true love's first kiss with Prince Edward.

330. HISTRIONIC:

Excessively dramatic; a deliberate display of emotion

In the movie "Clueless," Mr. Hall distributes report cards to his first period class. Travis takes one look at his dismal grades and tries to jump out of the ground floor window. But Mr. Hall recognizes a HISTRIONIC performance when he sees one. The veteran teacher pulls Travis away from the window saying, "could the suicide attempts please be postponed till the next period."

331. PLACATE:

To soothe or calm; appease

Travis is not the only one to receive low grades (see Word 330). Cher reacts with great CONSTERNATION (Word 318) when she discovers that Mr. Hall has given her a C in debate. Cher skillfully PLACATES her father by claiming that "some teachers are trying to low-ball me." As the daughter of a high-powered lawyer, Cher views her grades as "a first offer" and promises to use them as "a jumping off point to start negotiations." PLACATED by Cher's strategy, her father agrees to wait. His patience is rewarded when Cher successfully argues her way from a C to an A-.

332. ESCHEW:

To avoid; shun; stay clear of

What do the beatniks of the 1950's and the hippies of the 1960's have in common? Both ESCHEWED the conventional middle-class lifestyle of their times. The beatniks ESCHEWED conformity and materialism.

Preferring to pursue a more commercial lifestyle, the hippies ESCHEWED commercialism and competition.

333. STOPGAP:
A temporary solution designed to meet an urgent need

The Great Depression confronted the United States with an UNPRECEDENTED (Word 249) economic crisis. During the famous Hundred Days, Congress responded by passing a series of emergency bills. Critics promptly attacked the National Industrial Recovery Act (NIRA), the Agricultural Adjustment Act (AAA) and other New Deal programs by calling them STOPGAP measures that at best provided only short-term relief. Historians now take a more balanced view arguing that the New Deal included both WATERSHED laws (Word 232) and STOPGAP programs that MITIGATED (Word 31) but did not end the Depression.

334. FLOTSAM:
The floating wreckage of a ship; debris

Did you see "Pirates of the Caribbean: Dead Man's Chest?" According to legend, the Kraken was a huge, many armed creature that could reach as high as the top of a sailing ship's main mast. The Kraken attacked a ship by wrapping its tentacles around the hull, causing it to capsize, and leaving only scattered FLOTSAM behind.

While FLOTSAM typically refers to floating wreckage, it can also refer to cosmic debris. For example, the asteroid Eugenia is one of thousands of bits of cosmic FLOTSAM in the great asteroid belt between the orbits of the planets Mars and Jupiter.

335. RESTITUTION:
The act of making good or compensating for a loss, damage or injury

In 1942, the U.S. Army's Western Defense Command ordered the forced evacuation of 110,000 Japanese Americans living on the Pacific Coast. Fearing that they might act as SABOTEURS (subversive agents) for Japan, the government ordered Japanese Americans to pack up their belongings and move to "relocation centers" hastily erected farther inland. Forty-six years later, the U.S. government officially apologized for its action and approved a RESTITUTION payment of $20,000 to each camp survivor.

336. CHURLISH, SULLEN, SURLY:
All three mean ill-tempered; rude; lacking civility

What do Landon Carter ("A Walk to Remember") and Hancock ("Hancock") have in common? Both are initially CHURLISH characters who ultimately become more mature. In the opening scenes of "A Walk to Remember," Landon is a CHURLISH teenager who hangs out with an equally SULLEN group of immature friends who lack direction, goals and any form of faith. In the opening scenes of "Hancock," Hancock is a SURLY superhero who is DISHEVELED (unkempt, messy), perpetually drunk and despised by little children.

337. DISQUIETING:
Disturbing; upsetting; causing unease

In the movie "A Walk to Remember," Landon falls in love with Jamie and is transformed from a CHURLISH boor into a sensitive person who is beginning to find himself (see Word 336). But Landon receives a severe jolt when Jamie reveals some very DISQUIETING information about her health. She has leukemia and has stopped responding to treatment. Although shocked by Jamie's DISQUIETING story, Landon's love nonetheless remains steadfast.

338. ORNATE:
Characterized by elaborate and expensive decorations; LAVISH

What do the French king Louis XIV and the American rapper 50 Cent have in common? The both have a PENCHANT (Word 62) for ORNATE decorations. Built by Louis XIV, the Versailles Palace was one of the most ORNATE palaces in the world. Its LAVISH Hall of Mirrors contained so much silver furniture that it was part of France's monetary reserve. 50 Cent's 48,000 square foot estate includes 19 bedrooms, 4 kitchens, a movie theatre, a full gym and 5 Jacuzzis. His ORNATE dining room features an $80,000 Baccarat crystal chandelier.

339. EXECRABLE, ODIOUS, REPUGNANT:
Detestable; repulsive; extremely bad

In the movie, "The Dark Knight," the Joker is a maniacal fiend who delights in committing EXECRABLE crimes that terrorize Gotham City.

Unlike most criminals, the Joker is not motivated by money or greed. Instead, he is a criminal mastermind who commits ODIOUS crimes for pleasure. A CALLOUS (Word 72) fiend who is DEVOID (Word 180) of any morality, the Joker gleefully takes pleasure in the chaos he creates. To the REPUGNANT clown prince of crime, a knife is preferable to a gun, since it enables the Joker to "savor the moment."

340. PERSPICACIOUS, PRESCIENT, DISCERNING:
All three words mean insightful and perceptive

What do the French political writer Alexis de Tocqueville and the Jedi Master Yoda have in common? Both were unusually PERSPICACIOUS. De Tocqueville visited the United States in 1831 and published his observations four years later. De Tocqueville PRESCIENTLY predicted that the debate over slavery would tear the Union apart and that the United States and Russia were destined to be rivals. Like de Tocqueville, Yoda was also an unusually DISCERNING observer of human nature. For example, Yoda was very PERSPICACIOUS when he realized that the young Anakin Skywalker could be seduced by the dark side of the Force. Yoda's PRESCIENT insight proved to be true when Anakin became the villainous Darth Vader.

341. ECLECTIC:
Choosing or using a variety of sources

A person with ECLECTIC taste in music would like Beethoven, Akon, Linkin Park, Rihanna, Carrie

Underwood, and Shakira. Similarly, a teacher with an ECLECTIC repertoire of lesson strategies would play DVDs, assign internet projects, hold debates and give lectures.

342. HIATUS:
An interruption in time or continuity; a break

During the 1980's, Harrison Ford starred in three hugely successful movies featuring the adventures of Indiana Jones. After a 19-year HIATUS, Indy finally returned as the world's best-known archaeologist in "Indiana Jones and the Kingdom of the Crystal Skull." Interestingly, executive producer George Lucas and director Steven Spielberg set Crystal Skull in 1957, exactly 19 years after the events in "Indiana Jones and the Last Crusade." Thus the HIATUS in the movies paralleled the HIATUS in the real-world life of Harrison Ford.

343. VERTIGINOUS:
Characterized or suffering from dizziness; VERTIGO

What do the films "Blair Witch Project" and "Cloverfield" have in common? Although fictional, both films are presented as documentaries pieced together from amateurish footage. As a result, both films left many movie goers feeling VERTIGINOUS. This VERTIGINOUS effect was particularly pronounced in "Cloverfield." Shot and edited to look like it was filmed with a hand-held camera, "Cloverfield" included numerous jump-cuts that created a sense of VERTIGO, especially among those who sat near the screen.

344. ESOTERIC and ARCANE:
Characterized by knowledge that is known only to a small group of specialists; obscure

Have you ever heard of the Resolute Desk located in the Oval Office of the White House? Most people know little or nothing about the desk. But Benjamin Franklin Gates is not a typical person. In the movies "National Treasure" and "National Treasure: Book of Secrets," Gates is a renowned treasure hunter who is a storehouse of ESOTERIC information. Ben demonstrated his knowledge of ARCANE facts when he explained that the Resolute Desk was made from wood taken from the British warship HMS Resolute and then given to President Hayes by Queen Victoria. Gates further demonstrated his knowledge of ESOTERIC details when he explained that Franklin Roosevelt placed a panel in front of the desk to prevent visitors from seeing his leg braces and wheelchair.

345. SUPERCILIOUS:
Haughty disdain, arrogant superiority

What do Lucius Malfoy in the Harry Potter SAGA (Word 198) and Cal in the movie "Titanic" have in common? Both demonstrated a SUPERCILIOUS attitude toward their so-called inferiors. Lucius Malfoy demonstrated a SUPERCILIOUS attitude toward Harry Potter and other "mudbloods" who were born of one "pureblood" parent and one Muggle parent. Cal demonstrated a SUPERCILIOUS attitude toward Jack and other third-class passengers in steerage.

346. CUPIDITY:

Excessive greed, especially for wealth; covetous

What do the goblins in Harry Potter and Daniel Plainview in the movie "There Will Be Blood" have in common? Both are known for their all-consuming CUPIDITY. Goblins are extremely greedy and will protect their money and valuables at all costs. Daniel Plainview is a heartless, hard-bargaining oil man who is blinded by CUPIDITY. Although he wins a fortune, Plainview loses his soul.

347. UNDERWRITE:

To assume financial responsibility for

The Bill and Melinda Gates Foundation is the largest charitable foundation in the world. Its endowment of $38.7 billion dollars enables the foundation to UNDERWRITE numerous projects in the United States and around the world. For example, the Gates Millennium Scholars fund UNDERWRITES a one billion dollar program to provide scholarships for outstanding minority students.

348. DISCOMFITED:

To make uneasy; to put into a state of embarrassment

In the movie "Princess Diaries," Mia is a shy tenth grade student who attends a private school in San Francisco. Mia is shocked when she discovers that she is heir to the throne of Genovia, a small European principality ruled by her grandmother Queen Clarisse. Convinced to attend "princess lessons," Mia feels DIS-COMFITED as she learns the etiquette of being a princess. Mia's feelings of DISCOMFITURE become even greater when she attends her school's annual beach party and is embarrassed both when Josh deliberately kisses her in front of a group of photographers and Lana helps photographers take pictures of her clad only in a towel.

349. TACITURN:
Habitually quiet; uncommunicative

Have you watched the movies "Clerks," Clerks II," "Chasing Amy," "Mall Rats," or "Jay and Silent Bob Strike Back?" All of these movies feature a character named Silent Bob. Silent Bob smokes too much, often wears a long coat and a backward baseball cap and as his nickname suggests he seldom talks and is thus TACITURN. Silent Bob usually relies on hand gestures and facial expressions to communicate his feelings. Although normally TACITURN, Silent Bob is very insightful on the few occasions when he speaks out.

350. SINECURE:
An office or position that requires little or no work and that usually provides an income

In the movie "Batman Begins," Bruce Wayne is a billionaire businessman who lives in Gotham City. To the world at large, Wayne holds a SINECURE at Wayne Enterprises that enables him to act as an irresponsible, SUPERFICIAL playboy (see Word 90) who lives off his family's personal fortune. Of course, this SINE-CURE and the Bruce Wayne persona are masks that enable Wayne to hide his secret identity as the Caped Crusader, Batman.

351. LUGUBRIOUS:
Sad and mournful music

In "Star Wars: Episode III Revenge of the Sith," Padme's death and funeral are accompanied by a LUGUBRIOUS musical score. Similarly, in "Titanic," the musicians play a LUGUBRIOUS hymn as the great but doomed ship slowly sinks into the Atlantic Ocean.

352. COSMOPOLITAN:
Worldly; sophisticated; open-minded and aware of the big picture

PROVINCIAL, PAROCHIAL, INSULAR:
Limited in perspective; narrow; restricted in scope and outlook

Pretend that you are the editor of a newspaper serving a community of 75,000 people. A local middle school teacher has just been named the city's "teacher of the year." At the same time, a story has just come into your office describing changing admission standards in the nation's top universities and colleges. Which story would you place on your paper's front page?

Your decision will probably depend upon whether you have a COSMOPOLITAN or a PROVINCIAL outlook. A COSMOPOLITAN editor would favor a "big picture" outlook and give precedence to the national story. A PROVINCIAL editor would favor a local and thus more narrow approach.

The contrast between COSMOPOLITAN and PROVINCIAL outlooks can be traced back to their origins. COSMOPOLITAN is derived from the Greek words *kosmos* or "world" and *polites* or "citizen." So a COSMOPOLITAN person is literally a citizen of the world. In contrast, a province is an outlying part of an empire or nation, so a PROVINCIAL person would have a more limited perspective. Note that PAROCHIAL and INSULAR are synonyms that refer to a narrow outlook. PAROCHIAL is derived from parish, a small administrative unit with just one pastor and INSULAR is derived from the Latin word *insula* meaning island.

353. FECUND:
Intellectually productive or inventive

What do George Lucas and J.K. Rowling have in common? Both have unusually FECUND imaginations. In his Star Wars SAGA (Word 198), George Lucas created a Galactic Empire populated by humans, alien creatures, robotic droids, Jedi Knights and Sith Lords. In her Harry Potter SAGA, J.K. Rowling created a secret magical world populated by wizards, witches, dragons, goblins, giants and elves.

354. OSTENTATIOUS:
Showy; intended to attract notice; pretentious

Wearing OSTENTATIOUS jewelry has a long history. Egyptian Pharaohs, European rulers, and Mughal sultans all enjoyed wearing OSTENTATIOUS jewelry. For example, Queen Elizabeth I's wardrobe included 2,000 velvet and jewel-encrusted gowns.

The passion for wearing OSTENTATIOUS jewelry has not gone out of fashion. Commonly referred to as "bling-bling," OSTENTATIOUS jewelry is a hallmark of hip-hop culture. For example, Rick Ross is well known for his OSTENTATIOUS jewelry. The "Big Boss" recently purchased a chain featuring a pendant with an image of himself. The eye-catching piece includes Ross' trademark shades and reportedly cost $200,000.

355. GUILE:
Treacherous cunning; skillful deceit

What do Supreme Chancellor Palpatine ("Star Wars: Revenge of the Sith"), King Edward I ("Braveheart") and Cher ("Clueless") all have in common? They all use GUILE to achieve their goals. Supreme Chancellor Palpatine uses GUILE to deceive Anakin, King Edward I uses GUILE to capture William Wallace and Cher uses GUILE to trick Mr. Hall into falling in love with Ms. Guise so that he will be blissfully happy and raise everyone's grades.

356. SANGUINE:
Cheerfully confident; optimistic

In the movie "Enchanted," Giselle is a beautiful maiden who lives in the IDYLLIC (Word 305) land of Andalasia. Giselle meets and falls in love with handsome Prince Edward. However, their marriage plans are THWART-ED (Word 68) when villainous Queen Narissa banishes Giselle to a place where there are no happily ever afters – Times Square in modern New York City. Despite this setback, Giselle remains surprisingly

SANGUINE. She is confident that Prince Edward will rescue her and take her back to Andalasia.

357. SCINTILLATING:
Sparkling; shining; brilliantly clever

Both critics and fans have LAUDED (Word 91) the late Heath Ledger for his SCINTILLATING performance as the Joker in "The Dark Knight." Ledger demonstrated a full command of his character as he completely immersed himself in the role of the psychopathic criminal. The SCINTILLATING scenes featuring confrontations between the Joker and Batman sparkled with an intense energy and TAUT (tightly drawn) drama. If, as many movie historians believe, a film is as good as its villain, then Heath Ledger's riveting and SCINTILLATING performance as the Joker creates an unforgettable cinematic experience.

358. PRISTINE:
Remaining in a pure state; uncorrupted by civilization

Sandwiched between Latin American giants Venezuela and Brazil, Guyana is a small country with a vital global asset. About 80 percent of the country is covered by a PRISTINE rainforest called the Guyana Shield. The Shield is one of only four intact PRISTINE rain forests left on the planet. It is home to 1,400 vertebrate species, 1,680 bird species, and some of the world's most endangered species including the jaguar, anaconda, and giant anteater. In a groundbreaking agreement, the government of Guyana announced that it will place over one million acres of PRISTINE rain-forest under the protection of a British-led international body in return for development aid.

359. RAMPANT:
Unrestrained; unchecked

While Guyana is taking steps to protect its rainforest, the once PRISTINE (Word 358) Amazon Rainforest is being dramatically reduced by RAMPANT development led by cattle ranchers and loggers. Unless this RAMPANT deforestation is ARRESTED (Word 251), the Amazon Rainforest will be reduced by 40 percent in the next twenty years. This will result in the irreversible loss of thousands of species of plants and animals.

360. PERNICIOUS:
Highly injurious; destructive; deadly

Francisco Santos, the Vice-President of Columbia, has launched an international campaign to warn people about the PERNICIOUS consequences of cocaine trafficking. To get his message across, Santos chose to make an example of Kate Moss, the British supermodel who was photographed allegedly snorting cocaine. "When she snorted a line of cocaine, she put land mines in Columbia, she killed people in Columbia, she displaced people in Columbia," Santos told a concerned audience. The PERNICIOUS consequences of cocaine trafficking also extend to the environment. "She destroyed the environment," Santos continued. "We have lost two million hectares (about 5 million acres) of PRISTINE (Word 358) rain forest to drug trafficking."

361. OBLIVIOUS:

Lacking conscious awareness; unmindful; unaware

Senator Stephen A. Douglas of Illinois was a brilliant and ambitious leader whom many thought could become President. But Douglas was also OBLIVIOUS to the intensity of popular opposition to the spread of slavery into the western territories. His ill-considered support of the Kansas-Nebraska Act created a firestorm that played a key role in causing both the Civil War and his own downfall.

Senator Douglas is not the only person to pay a price for being OBLIVIOUS to what others are feeling or thinking. For example, have you ever been unaware of your boyfriend's or girlfriend's feelings? If so, then like Senator Douglas you were being OBLIVIOUS.

362. REFRACTORY:

Obstinately resistant to authority or control

Do you believe that it is possible to create a utopian community? From the Puritan communities at Massachusetts Bay to the hippie communes in the 1960's, many people have tried and failed to create utopias. While there are many reasons why utopian communities have failed, the sheer REFRACTORI-NESS of human nature is a leading cause. Petty quarrels and jealous disputes provide all-too common examples of REFRACTORY behavior that undermines even the most ideal group goals.

363. GARRULOUS, VERBOSE, LOQUACIOUS:
Annoyingly talkative

What do Donkey in all three Shrek movies and Seth in "Superbad" have in common? Both are very GARRULOUS. Donkey often exasperates Shrek with his VERBOSE chatter. And Seth is so LOQUACIOUS that it is difficult to think of a time when he isn't talking.

364. CONVIVIAL:
Fond of feasting, drinking, and good company

What do the Deltas in "Animal House" and Ben Stone and his friends in "Knocked Up" have in common? They are both merry bands of CONVIVIAL slackers who love to eat, drink, and party. In fact, Ben and his CONVIVIAL buddies are really only slightly older versions of Bluto and his CONVIVIAL fraternity brothers.

365. BRUSQUE and CURT:
Abrupt in manner or speech; discourteously blunt

What do Donald Trump, Dr. House, and Montgomery bus driver J. F. Blake have in common? All three share the trait of being BRUSQUE. In the reality show "The Apprentice," Donald Trump is BRUSQUE when he tells each week's losing apprentice, "You're fired!" Dr. House ("House M.D.") is a medical genius who is very impatient and CURT with young doctors who misdiagnose an illness. And finally, J.F. Blake PRECIPITATED (Word 253) the Montgomery Bus Boycott when he CURTLY ordered Rosa Parks to give up her seat.

Testing Your Vocabulary

Each SAT contains 19 sentence completion questions that are primarily a test of your vocabulary. Each sentence completion will always have a key word or phrase that will lead you to the correct answer. Use the vocabulary from Chapters 6-10 to circle the answer to each of the following 10 sentence completion questions. You'll find answers and explanations on pages 125-126.

1. Good parenting groups denounced the YouTube video, finding it to be in _____ taste because it included repulsive images and profane language.

    (A) scintillating
    (B) discriminating
    (C) ornate
    (D) execrable
    (E) ineffable

2. The late Isaac Asimov is among the most _____ writers of all time, having written or edited over 500 books.

    (A) paranoid
    (B) sanguine
    (C) dilatory
    (D) prolific
    (E) censorious

3. Matthew was both _____ and _____: he was surly to the point of being rude and arrogant to the point of being obnoxious.

   (A) churlish .. supercilious
   (B) convivial .. imperious
   (C) curt .. histrionic
   (D) verbose .. didactic
   (E) refractory .. sanguine

4. Judy Chicago, an influential contemporary artist, is known for her _____ style which features an eccentric and highly individualistic interweaving of themes, imagery and materials.

   (A) pristine
   (B) lugubrious
   (C) idiosyncratic
   (D) apocryphal
   (E) vacuous

5. Parties and other social gatherings benefit from having _____ hosts who provide entertaining company, delicious food and lively conversation.

   (A) truculent
   (B) refractory
   (C) oblivious
   (D) brusque
   (E) convivial

6. Like all _____ literature, *Aesop's Fables* was intended to teach important moral lessons and inculcate key cultural values.

    (A) didactic
    (B) histrionic
    (C) pristine
    (D) superfluous
    (E) empirical

7. In temperament the two leaders were very different: Janice was convivial, talkative and at times even _____; in contrast, Sherece was unassuming, guarded and at times even _____.

    (A) surly .. sullen
    (B) garrulous .. taciturn
    (C) verbose .. effusive
    (D) imperious .. egalitarian
    (E) obstreperous .. censorious

8. Although Caravaggio was a key figure in Rome's emerging new Baroque style of art, he nevertheless perceived himself as being _____ figure with little influence.

    (A) a vital
    (B) a marginal
    (C) an ungainly
    (D) an epic
    (E) a watershed

9. Since many successful composers draw their inspiration from a variety of cultures, styles and disciplines, their approach could best be called _____.

(A) refractory
(B) vertiginous
(C) histrionic
(D) idyllic
(E) eclectic

10. Minimalist sculptors renounced _____ decorations in favor of an extremely spare style that emphasized basic geometric figures.

(A) stopgap
(B) execrable
(C) redolent
(D) ornate
(E) insular

Answers and Explanations

1. **D**

   The question asks you to find a word describing a video that contains "repulsive images and profane language." The correct answer is EXECRABLE (Word 339).

2. **D**

   The question asks you to find a word that describes an author who has written or edited over 500 books. The correct answer is PROLIFIC (Word 322).

3. **A**

   The question asks you to find a first word that means "surly" and a second word that means "arrogant." The correct answer is CHURLISH (Word 336) and SUPERCILIOUS (Word 345).

4. **C**

   The question asks you to find a word that describes an artist who is "eccentric" and "highly individualistic." The correct answer is IDIOSYNCRATIC (Word 315).

5. **E**

   The question asks you to find a word describing a host who provides "entertaining company, delicious food and a lively atmosphere." The correct answer is CONVIVIAL (Word 364).

6. A

The question asks you to find a word that means "to teach important moral lessons and inculcate key cultural values." The correct answer is DIDACTIC (Word 319).

7. B

The question asks you to find a first word that means "talkative" and a second word describing a "very different" person who is "guarded." The correct answer is GARRULOUS (Word 363) and TACITURN (Word 349).

8. B

The question asks you to find a word that is the opposite of "key figure" and is consistent with having "little influence." The correct answer is MARGINAL (Word 325).

9. E

The question asks you to find a word that means "variety." The correct answer is ECLECTIC (Word 341).

10. D

The question asks you to find a word that is the opposite of having "a spare style" and "basic geometric forms." The correct answer is ORNATE (Word 338).

Final Review

Testing Your Vocabulary: Final Review

The following 10 sentence completion and 5 critical reading questions are designed to give you practice using your knowledge of the core vocabulary in Volume 1 and the toughest words in Volume 2. As always, each sentence completion will have a key word or phrase that will lead you to the correct answer and make sure to circle your answer. You'll find answers and explanations on pages 134-137.

Sentence Completion

1. Art teachers enthusiastically _____ the new clay saying that its extraordinary _____ enabled students to mold it into almost any shape.

    (A) touted .. buoyancy
    (B) extolled .. plasticity
    (C) expurgated .. eccentricity
    (D) disparaged .. malleability
    (E) reaffirmed .. longevity

2. Olivia was both _____ and _____: she gave generously to charities but was very thrifty when it came to her personal spending.

    (A) cosmopolitan .. parochial
    (B) philanthropic .. venal
    (C) munificent .. parsimonious
    (D) eclectic .. hackneyed
    (E) affable .. craven

3. Theatre producers rejected the impenetrably dense screenplay saying that its _____ rendered it unsuitable for even its most sophisticated and _____ patrons.

    (A) poignancy .. pompous
    (B) superficiality .. clairvoyance
    (C) subtlety .. pragmatic
    (D) opacity .. cosmopolitan
    (E) serendipity .. discerning

4. The controversial YouTube video elicited _____ responses: some posts were derisive while other were _____.

    (A) antithetical .. laudatory
    (B) complementary .. dismissive
    (C) fleeting .. maudlin
    (D) nostalgic .. anguished
    (E) unprecedented .. curt

5. The governor's emergency measures were intended as _____, a temporary expedient that called for voluntary water conservation until permanent laws could be put into place.

    (A) a metaphor
    (B) an anecdote
    (C) a conundrum
    (D) an inquisition
    (E) a stopgap

6. Abigail was an affable and _____ woman; she had none of her sister's _____.

    (A) indomitable .. tenacity
    (B) churlish .. amiability
    (C) sullen .. belligerence
    (D) obstinate .. recalcitrance
    (E) genial .. truculence

7.   Those unfriendly critics who preferred opera that was _____ and melodious found the music of Christopher Markham jarring and warned that his influence on opera would be _____.

   (A)   obstreperous .. lugubrious
   (B)   provocative .. platitudinous
   (C)   scintillating .. superfluous
   (D)   euphonious .. pernicious
   (E)   cacophonous .. perfidious

8.   Emily's _____ was the inverse of her brother's _____: she was bold to a fault, while he was overly _____.

   (A)   audacity .. circumspect
   (B)   munificence .. parsimonious
   (C)   belligerence .. truculent
   (D)   complaisance .. petulant
   (E)   verbosity .. loquacious

9.   Many scientists view the precipitous decline in the populations of both polar bears and penguins as a _____: an early warning of the deleterious consequences of global warming.

   (A)   pretext
   (B)   caricature
   (C)   portent
   (D)   paradigm
   (E)   synopsis

10. The late Isaac Asimov was both _____ and
_____: he wrote voluminously while
maintaining exacting standards of research.

    (A) didactic .. idiosyncratic
    (B) prolific .. meticulous
    (C) histrionic .. censorious
    (D) discerning .. disquieting
    (E) eclectic .. superficial

Critical Reading

I realized from the beginning that Mr. Williams was a
born teacher. He combined a profound knowledge of
literature with an intuitive understanding of teenage
students. And most of all he excelled in telling
entertaining anecdotes that illustrated his key points.

11. As described by the author, Mr. Williams comes
across as

    (A) a confused dilettante
    (B) a talented raconteur
    (C) a revered iconoclast
    (D) an impassioned demagogue
    (E) a clever charlatan

A stunning lack of attention to plot and dialogue are
by far the most egregious flaws that plague a movie
that should never have been filmed let alone released.

12. The tone of this sentence is best described as

    (A) scathing
    (B) tempered
    (C) archaic
    (D) convivial
    (E) ambiguous

Art historian Marilyn Stokestad argues that in all of known history only three major artists appeared on the scene by themselves: fourteenth century Renaissance artist Giotto, seventeenth century Baroque artist Caravaggio, and twentieth century Cubist artist Picasso. Every other artist was part of a movement or specific style.

13. The passage indicates that Giotto, Caravaggio and Picasso are best viewed as

    (A)   controversial pundits
    (B)   polarizing contemporaries
    (C)   inept novices
    (D)   historical anomalies
    (E)   superficial sycophants

As a dedicated reformer, I.N. Stokes contended against dumbbell tenements calling them "dirty, overcrowded, degraded places run by exploitive landlords." Stokes' housing reform efforts culminated when, serving on the New York State Tenement House Commission, he co-authored the Tenement House Law of 1901, which required tenements to have a host of new features, including deep backyards, larger rooms, and broad side-courts.

14. I.N. Stokes attitude toward dumbbell apartments is best described as

    (A)   enlightened advocacy
    (B)   resolute opposition
    (C)   paralyzing ambivalence
    (D)   tempered acquiescence
    (E)   nostalgic reminiscence

At that time, I was a traveling reporter assigned to Frederickson's Senate campaign. As the days turned into weeks, I heard his basic stump speech dozens of times. I soon became bored as Frederickson endlessly repeated clichés and slogans about standing up to the Russians, cutting government waste and building a new and better America.

15. The author believed that Frederickson's speeches were

    (A) scintillating
    (B) divisive
    (C) truculent
    (D) supercilious
    (E) trite

Answers and Explanations

1.   B

The question asks you to find a positive first word and a second word that is consistent with the phrase "mold it into almost any shape." The correct answer is EXTOLLED (Word 91) and PLASTICITY (Word 302). Note that in Choice D while malleability (Word 302) works for the second blank, disparaged (Word 93) is a negative word that is not consistent with the key word "enthusiastically."

2.   C

The question asks you to find a first word that is consistent with giving "generously" to charities and a second word that is consistent with being "thrifty" in her personal spending. The correct answer is MUNIFICENT (Word 222) and PARSIMONIOUS (Word 223).

3.   D

The question asks you to find a first word that means "impenetrably dense" and a second word that is consistent with "sophisticated." The correct answer is OPACITY (Word 275) and COSMOPOLITAN (Word 352).

4.   A

The question asks you to find a first word that means opposite since the second word must be an antonym of the negative word "derisive." The correct answer is ANTITHETICAL (Word 33) and LAUDATORY (Word 91).

5. **E**

The question asks you to find a word that is consistent with the key phrase "temporary expedient." The correct answer is STOPGAP (Word 333).

6. **E**

The question asks you to find a positive first word that is a synonym of "affable" and a second word that is an antonym of the first word. The correct answer is GENIAL (Word 18) and TRUCULENCE (Word 270).

7. **D**

The question asks you to find a first word that is a synonym of melodious and a negative second word describing how "unfriendly critics" would view the influence of Markham's "jarring" music. The correct answer is EUPHONIOUS (Word 241) and PERNICIOUS (Word 360).

8. **A**

The question asks you to find a first word that means "bold" and a second word that is the "inverse" or opposite of "bold." The correct answer is AUDACITY (Word 9) and CIRCUMSPECT (Word 187).

9. **C**

The question asks you to find a word that is consistent with the key phrase "an early warning." The correct answer is PORTENT (Word 286).

10. B

The question asks you to find a first word that is consistent with writing "voluminously" and a second word that means to maintain "exacting standards of research." The correct answer is PROLIFIC (Word 322) and METICULOUS (Word 8).

11. B

The passage describes Mr. Williams as a "born teacher" who excels "in telling entertaining anecdotes." The correct answer is therefore B, since "a talented RACONTEUR" (Word 106) is a person who excels in telling anecdotes.

12. A

The passage pinpoints "egregious flaws" in a movie that "should never have been filmed." Since the author's tone is harshly critical, the correct answer is A, "SCATHING" (Word 266).

13. D

The passage tells you that Giotto, Caravaggio and Picasso all "appeared on the scene by themselves" and were not "part of a movement or specific style." Since the three artists were atypical the correct answer is D, "historical ANOMALIES" (Word 2).

14. B

The passage tells you that I.N. Stokes was a "dedicated reformer" who "contended against dumbbell tenements." Since "dedicated" supports "resolute" and "contended against" supports "opposition," the correct answer is B, "RESOLUTE (Word 315) opposition."

15. **E**

The passage tells you that Frederickson's "endlessly repeated clichés and slogans" bored the author. Since "clichés and slogans" are unoriginal and overused words, the correct answer is E, "TRITE" (Word 36).

Fast Review

Quick Definitions

Volume 2 contains 175 words each of which is illustrated with vivid pop culture and historic examples. The Fast Review is designed to provide you with an easy and efficient way to review the definition of each of these words. I recommend that you put a check beside each word that you know. That way you can quickly identify the words that you are having trouble remembering. Focus on each hard to remember word by going over its definition, taking another look at the examples in your book and by trying to come up with your own memory tip. For example, take a close look at Word 311, VITUPERATIVE. Mentally take out the letters TUP and now you have VIPER. A viper is a large venomous snake. The word VITUPERATIVE includes this sense of being vicious and venomous. A VITUPERATIVE critic is filled with bitter criticisms.

Good luck with your review. Remember, don't expect to learn all of these words at once. Frequent repetition is the best way to learn and remember new words.

CHAPTER 6: KEY LITERARY TERMS

191. SYNOPSIS – a brief summary
192. SIMILE – a figure of speech using like or as to compare two unlike things
193. METAPHOR – a figure of speech comparing two unlike things
194. IRONY – things are not what they are said to be or what they seem
195. SATIRE – a work that ridicules human vices and foibles
196. HYPERBOLE – an exaggeration is used for emphasis or effect
197. CARICATURE – a deliberately exaggerated portrait
198. EPIC – a long narrative poem
    SAGA – a long narrative story
199. EUPHONY – soothing, pleasant sound
    CACOPHONY – jarring, grating sound
200. FORESHADOW – suggest or indicate a future action; presage
201. SUBPLOT – a secondary plot in fiction or drama
202. MEMOIR – a personal journal
203. ANECDOTE – a short account of an interesting incident
204. EULOGY – a laudatory speech or written tribute
205. ALLUSION – a indirect or brief reference to a person, place or event

CHAPTER 7: KEY WORDS FROM SCIENCE AND THE SOCIAL SCIENCES

206. CATALYST – an agent that provokes or triggers a change

207. CAUSTIC – a stinging or bitter remark

208. SYNTHETIC – produced artificially

209. OSMOSIS – a gradual often unconscious process of assimilation

210. SEDENTARY – settled; not mobile

211. VIRULENT – very toxic or poisonous

212. EMPIRICAL – guided by practical experience and not theory

213. ENTOMOLOGY – the scientific study of insects

214. GESTATE – to conceive and develop in the mind

215. PARADIGM – a framework or model of thought

216. ENTREPRENEUR – a person who organizes and runs a business

217. LUCRATIVE – very profitable

218. EXTRAVAGANT - excessive

219. AVARICE – excessive greed

220. GLUT, PLETHORA, SURFEIT – a surplus
PAUCITY – a shortage

221. DESTITUTE, IMPOVERISHED, INDIGENT – very poor
AFFLUENT and OPULENT – very wealthy

222. MUNIFICENT – very generous

223. PARSIMONIOUS – excessively cheap; stingy

224. DEPRECIATION – a decrease in value

225. REMUNERATE – to compensate; a salary
226. ACCORD – a formal agreement
227. ENLIGHTEN – to illuminate
228. APPEASEMENT – to grant concessions to maintain peace
229. NULLIFY – to make null; declare invalid
230. TRIUMVIRATE – a group of three leaders
231. PRETEXT – an excuse; an alleged cause
232. WATERSHED – a critical turning point
233. CONSENSUS – a general agreement
234. AUTOCRAT and DESPOT – a ruler with unlimited power
235. MANIFESTO – a public declaration of beliefs
236. ENFRANCHISE – to receive the right to vote
    DISENFRANCHISE – to lose the right to vote
237. COERCE – to compel someone to do something
238. EGALITARIAN – belief in a society based upon equality
239. BELLIGERENT – hostile and aggressive; warlike
240. INQUISITION – a severe interrogation; a systematic questioning
241. AMELIORATE – to make better
    EXACERBATE – to make worse
242. CONTIGUOUS – sharing an edge or boundary; touching
243. DESICCATE – to thoroughly dry out; totally arid
244. PERTINENT – relevant and to the point
245. COMPLICITY – association or participation in a wrongful act

246. EXONERATE and EXCULPATE – to free from blame or guilt

247. INDISPUTABLE – not open to question; irrefutable

248. PRECEDENT – an action or decision that serves as an example

249. UNPRECEDENTED – without a previous example

250. MALFEASANCE – misconduct or wrongdoing by a public official

CHAPTER 8: WORDS WITH MULTIPLE MEANINGS

251. ARREST – to bring to a stop; halt
252. GRAVITY – a serious situation or problem
253. PRECIPITATE – a result or outcome of an action
254. RELIEF – elevation of a land surface
255. CHECK – to restrain; halt; contain
256. FLAG – to become weak or feeble; to lose interest
257. DISCRIMINATING – selective or refined taste
258. ECLIPSE – overshadow; surpass
259. COIN – to devise a new word or phrase
260. STOCK – a stereotypical or formulaic character
261. CURRENCY – general acceptance or use
262. BENT – a strong tendency; a leaning or inclination
263. COURT – to attempt to gain the favor or support of a person or group
264. NEGOTIATE – to successfully travel through, around or over an obstacle
265. TEMPER – to soften; moderate

CHAPTER 9: THE TOUGHEST WORDS – PART I

266. SCATHING – harshly critical
267. QUIESCENT – inactive; very quiet
268. PROVISIONAL - temporary
269. LURID – sensational; shocking
270. TRUCULENT and PUGNACIOUS – defiantly aggressive; eager to fight
271. PROPITIATE – to appease; conciliate
272. ÉLAN – great enthusiasm
273. PERFUNCTORY – performed in a mechanical, spiritless manner
274. APLOMB – admirable poise under pressure
275. OPACITY – impenetrably dense; hard to understand
276. CRAVEN - cowardly
277. VENAL – corrupt; open to bribery
278. LICENTIOUS and DISSOLUTE – immoral; debauched
279. NOXIOUS – harmful; injurious to physical, mental or moral health
280. SUPERFLUOUS – unnecessary; extra
281. DUPLICITOUS – deliberate deceptiveness
282. PROFLIGATE – very wasteful, especially of time and money
283. EPIPHANY – a sudden realization
284. INSIDIOUS – causing harm in a subtle or stealthy manner; devious

285. VACUOUS – empty; lacking serious purpose

286. HARBINGER, PORTENT, PRESAGE – an omen that something will happen

287. BELEAGUER – to be beset with problems

288. BURGEON – to rapidly grow and expand

289. IMPERIOUS – domineering and arrogant

290. PETULANT – peevish; irritable

291. COMPLAISANT and AFFABLE – agreeable; amiable

292. FAWN – to behave in a servile manner; subservient

293. OBDURATE and INTRACTABLE – very stubborn; unyielding

294. REDOLENT – exuding fragrance

295. CHICANERY – deception by artful subterfuge; deliberate trickery

296. CONUNDRUM – a difficult problem; a dilemma with no easy solution

297. SLIGHT – a disrespectful or disparaging remark; a put down

298. CAPITULATE – to surrender; comply without protest

299. DISHEARTENING – very discouraged

300. APOCRYPHAL – of questionable authenticity

301. MAGISTERIAL – learned and authoritative

302. PLASTICITY, MALLEABLE, PLIABLE – can be molded into any shape

303. CHAGRIN – feeling of distress caused by humiliation or embarrassment

304. OBSTREPEROUS – nosily and stubbornly defiant; boisterous
305. IDYLLIC – charmingly simple and carefree
306. DILAPIDATED – broken-down; in deplorable condition
307. EXTEMPORIZE and IMPROVISE – to speak without notes
308. MYRIAD – many; numerous
309. UNGAINLY – awkward; clumsy
310. DILATORY – habitually late; tardy
311. VITUPERATIVE and VITRIOLIC – bitter criticism
312. DISCORDANT – a note of disharmony
313. PERFIDIOUS – treacherous; traitorous
314. SUPINE – lying on one's back
315. INDOMITABLE and RESOLUTE – very determined

CHAPTER 10: THE TOUGHEST WORDS – PART II

316. IDIOSYNCRASY – a trait or mannerism peculiar to an individual
317. CENSORIOUS – highly critical
318. CONSTERNATION – a state of great dismay and confusion
319. DIDACTIC – intended to provide instruction
320. ELUCIDATE – to make clear or plain
321. EFFUSIVE – unrestrained praise
322. PROLIFIC – very productive
323. FUROR – a general commotion; an uproar
324. PARANOIA – irrational fear
325. MARGINAL – of secondary importance; not central
326. OBFUSCATE – to deliberately confuse
327. FLUMMOX – to confuse; perplex
328. SPATE – a large number or amount
329. INEFFABLE – a feeling that cannot be put into words
330. HISTRIONIC – excessively dramatic
331. PLACATE – to soothe or calm
332. ESCHEW – to avoid
333. STOPGAP – a temporary solution
334. FLOTSAM – floating wreckage; debris
335. RESTITUTION – compensating for a loss
336. CHURLISH, SULLEN, SURLY – ill-tempered; rude

337. DISQUIETING – disturbing; upsetting; causing unease

338. ORNATE – characterized by elaborate and expensive decorations; lavish

339. EXECRABLE, ODIOUS, REPUGNANT – detestable and repulsive

340. PERSPICACIOUS, PRESCIENT, DISCERNING – very insightful

341. ECLECTIC – using a variety of sources

342. HIATUS – an interruption in time or continuity; a break

343. VERTIGINOUS - dizziness

344. ESOTERIC and ARCANE – obscure information known by a few people

345. SUPERCILIOUS – haughty and arrogant

346. CUPIDITY – excessive greed

347. UNDERWRITE – to assume financial responsibility for a project

348. DISCOMFITED – to make uneasy; state of embarrassment

349. TACITURN – habitually quiet

350. SINECURE – a job that provides income but requires little work

351. LUGUBRIOUS – sad and mournful music

352. COSMOPOLITAN – worldly; sophisticated
PROVINCIAL, PAROCHIAL, INSULAR – isolated from the mainstream

353. FECUND – intellectually productive or inventive

354. OSTENTATIOUS - showy

355. GUILE – treacherous cunning; skillful deceit

356. SANGUINE – cheerfully confident; optimistic

357. SCINTILLATING – sparkling; shining

358. PRISTINE – pure and uncorrupted

359. RAMPANT – unrestrained; unchecked

360. PERNICIOUS – highly injurious; destructive

361. OBLIVIOUS - unaware

362. REFRACTORY – obstinately resistant to authority or control

363. GARRULOUS, VERBOSE, LOQUACIOUS – very talkative

364. CONVIVIAL – fond of feasting, drinking and good company

365. BRUSQUE and CURT – abrupt; discourteously blunt

Index

Word	*Page*
Accord	33, 78
Acquiesce	38
Adroit	79
Affable	80, 88
Affluent	27, 30, 99
Allure	26
Allusion	9, 10
Ambiguity	100
Ameliorate	40, 41
Anecdote	1, 8, 9
Aplomb	73, 83
Apocryphal	84, 85
Appeasement	33, 34
Arcane	111
Archipelago	41
Arrest	54, 78, 118
Autocrat	36, 37, 39
Avarice	28, 29
Beleaguer	78, 79
Belligerent	39
Bent	59
Boorish	83, 98
Brusque	120
Burgeon	69, 79
Cacophony	6, 7
Callous	109
Candid	8
Capitulate	69, 83, 84
Capricious	7
Caricature	1, 5

Index

Catalyst.. 20
Caustic..20, 21
Censorious 98
Chagrin.. 86
Check...53, 55, 56
Chicanery 82
Churlish.. 97, 107, 108
Coerce.. 38
Coin 53, 57, 58, 71
Complaisant 80
Complicity..42, 43
Connoisseur 57
Consensus 36, 88
Consternation 99, 105
Contiguous...41
Conundrum... 82
Convivial 120
Convoluted..104
Corpulent 4
Cosmopolitan.. 114, 115
Court 60
Craven 74
Cupidity... 112
Currency...58, 59
Curt 120

Dearth 29
Debunk.. 83
Deft.. 100
Depreciation...32
Desiccate 41, 42
Despot..36, 37
Destitute... 30
Devoid 109

Didactic 97, 99
Dilapidated...87
Dilatory 69, 89
Diminutive 23
Discerning...109
Discomfited 112, 113
Discordant.. 90
Discriminating 56, 57
Disenfranchise 38
Disheartening.. 84
Disheveled..107
Disquieting...41, 108
Duplicitous...76

Eclectic 97, 109, 110
Eclipse...57
Effusive 100
Egalitarian.. 39
Élan 72
Elated 83
Elucidate 97, 100
Empirical... 24
Enfranchise 38
Enigmatic 10
Enlighten... 33, 83
Entomology..24, 25
Entrepreneur 27
Epic 3, 6, 100
Epiphany..77
Erroneous... 26
Eschew 105, 106
Esoteric 90, 111
Eulogy 9
Euphony..6, 7

Index

Exacerbate..40, 41
Exculpate.. 43
Execrable...43, 108
Exonerate 43
Extemporize 87
Extravagant 5, 28

Fawn..81
Fecund... 115
Fiasco 80
Flag...53, 56
Flotsam 106, 107
Flummox..104
Foreshadow..7
Furor 101
Futile 38, 89

Garrulous 120
Gestate 25
Glut... 29
Gravity..54
Guile 116

Harbinger..78
Hedonist...31, 98
Heresy 40
Hiatus.. 110
Histrionic 105
Hyperbole...5

Idiosyncrasy.. 98
Idyllic 87, 116
Imperious..79
Implacable...59
Impoverished 30, 37

Improvise 87, 88
Indigent... 30
Indignant 37
Indisputable 43
Indomitable..91
Indulgent..31
Ineffable 104
Inept..21, 89
Innocuous 90
Inquisition... 40
Insidious 77
Insular.. 114, 115
Insurmountable 79
Intractable...81
Intrepid 27
Irony..3, 4

Laud 100, 117
Lavish 108
Licentious..75
Loquacious 120
Lucrative 27, 28, 44
Lugubrious 114
Lurid.. 71

Magisterial 85
Malevolent 59
Malfeasance 45
Malleable.. 85
Manifesto 37
Marginal...102
Memoir... 8
Metaphor..3
Mitigate 61, 106

Index

Munificent..30, 31
Myriad.. 36, 88

Negotiate.. 60
Noxious 75
Nullify... 34

Obdurate 81
Obfuscate 103, 104
Oblivious 37, 119
Obstreperous... 86
Odious...108, 109
Opacity 73, 74
Opulent 30
Ornate 108
Osmosis.. 22, 89
Ostentatious... 115, 116

Panache..27, 76
Paradigm...25, 26
Paranoia...102
Parochial 114, 115
Parsimonious 31, 76
Paucity.. 29, 30
Penchant 98, 108
Perfidious...90, 91
Perfunctory 72, 73
Pernicious 118
Perspicacious 109
Pertinent 42, 83
Petulant.. 80
Philanthropist 88
Placate..105
Plasticity.. 85, 86
Plethora... 29

Pliable.. 85, 86
Portent 78
Pragmatic 26
Precedent 44
Precipitate 32, 55, 120
Précis..2
Presage 7, 78
Prescient.. 41, 109
Pretext 35
Pristine 117, 118
Prodigious 28
Profligate..76
Prolific.. 101
Propitiate 72
Provincial 114, 115
Provisional 70, 71
Pugnacious... 71

Quiescent 70

Rampant.................................... 118
Redolent..81
Refractory 97, 119
Regressed 5
Relief 55
Remunerate...32
Repugnant...................................108, 109
Resolute 79, 91
Restitution 107

Saboteur 107
Saga 6, 102, 111, 115
Sage 83
Sanguine................................... 116, 117
Satire 4

Index

Scathing...70
Scintillating...97, 117
Sedentary 22
Simile 2
Sinecure 113
Skeptic.. 43
Slight 83
Spate..104
Spurious 84
Stock... 58
Stopgap 88, 106
Subplot..7
Sullen 107
Supercilious 86, 111
Superficial 78, 113
Superfluous...75, 76
Supine 91
Surfeit... 29, 30
Surly 86, 107
Synopsis 2
Synthetic 21

Taciturn... 113
Taut 117
Temper...61
Thwart... 116
Tirade 59
Trite.. 58
Triumvirate 34, 35
Truculent...71

Undaunted 98
Underwrite.. 112
Ungainly...88, 89

Unorthodox 99
Unprecedented 44, 75, 106

Vacuous 78
Venal 74
Verbose 120
Vertiginous 100, 110
Viable 88
Virulent 23
Vitriolic 89, 90
Vituperative 89, 90, 139

Waft 81
Watershed 35, 36, 106

Printed in the United States
222110BV00001B/91/P